Pathways to Bliss
A SKELETON KEY STUDY GUIDE

PATHWAYS *to* BLISS

A SKELETON KEY STUDY GUIDE

by

BRADLEY OLSON, PhD

Copyright © 2023 Joseph Campbell Foundation

All rights reserved. No part of this publication may be reproduced, distributed, or transmitted in any form or by any means, including photocopying, recording, or other electronic or mechanical methods, without the prior written permission of the publisher, except in the case of brief quotations embodied in critical reviews and certain other noncommercial uses permitted by copyright law. For permission requests, please contact the Joseph Campbell Foundation's Rights and Permissions Manager at rights@jcf.org.

ISBN: 978-1-61178-039-0

Front cover image detail from *Madonna of the Rocks* by Leonardo da Vinci

Book design by *the*BookDesigners

First printing edition 2023

www.jcf.org

Contents

About *The Collected Works of Joseph Campbell* and the Joseph Campbell Foundation Skeleton Key Study Guide Series 1

How to Use This Study Guide 3

Skeleton Key Study Guide Introduction................ 5

CHAPTER I
The Necessity of Rites 21

CHAPTER II
Myth Through Time 37

CHAPTER III
Society and Symbol 57

CHAPTER IV
Myth and the Self 79

CHAPTER V
Personal Myth 101

CHAPTER VI
The Self as Hero............................... 121

CHAPTER VII
Dialogues..................................... 137

Final Thoughts from Bradley Olson, PhD 153

About Joseph Campbell 155

About the Author 157

About the Joseph Campbell Foundation 158

About
The Collected Works of Joseph Campbell
AND THE JOSEPH CAMPBELL FOUNDATION SKELETON KEY STUDY GUIDE SERIES

At his death in 1987, Joseph Campbell left a significant body of published work that explored his lifelong passion for myths and symbols from many cultures. He also left a large volume of unreleased work: uncollected articles, notes, letters, and diaries, as well as audio- and videotape recorded lectures.

The Joseph Campbell Foundation was founded in 1991 to preserve, promote, and perpetuate Campbell's work. The Foundation has undertaken to archive his papers and recordings in digital format, and to publish previously unavailable material and out-of-print works as *The Collected Works of Joseph Campbell*.

The Foundation is now also publishing this series of Skeleton Key Study Guides to accompany selected titles in the *Collected Works*. We intend study guides such as this one to provide entry points into Campbell's ideas for students and for others new to Campbell studies. We hope that Campbell's work and his way of working inspire you to bring new creativity, mythic awareness, and psychological depth to your own work, as they have already done for so many.

How to Use This Study Guide

A skeleton key can open many locks because it has been filed down to only the essentials. This study guide opens *Pathways to Bliss: Mythology and Personal Transformation* the same way. Each chapter of the study guide focuses on a corresponding chapter in *Pathways to Bliss*. In each chapter, you'll find a summary of the *Pathways* chapter, section by section, followed by points of interest in that chapter, as well as complementary reading lists. Chapters close with a selection of discussion questions, essay topics, and creative prompts. Our vision is that this study guide unlocks *Pathways to Bliss* for you, whether you are new to the material or deepening your relationship with it.

CITATIONS FROM *PATHWAYS TO BLISS*

Whenever this study guide quotes directly from *Pathways to Bliss: Mythology and Personal Transformation*, the text includes footnotes that contain page numbers on which you can find the original citation. These page numbers refer to the edition published in 2004 by New World Library.

Campbell, Joseph. *Pathways to Bliss: Mythology and Personal Transformation*. New World Library, 2004.

CITATIONS FROM *THE COLLECTED WORKS OF C.G. JUNG*

When this Skeleton Key Study Guide quotes from *The Collected Works of C.G. Jung*, citations will reference paragraph numbers rather than page numbers.

SKELETON KEY STUDY GUIDE
INTRODUCTION

Joseph Campbell (1904–1987) was a writer, mythologist, and professor of literature at Sarah Lawrence College (from 1934 to 1972). He became famous for a Bill Moyers interview on PBS called *The Power of Myth*. His seminal 1949 book, *The Hero with a Thousand Faces*, has influenced, directly or indirectly, screenwriters and novelists as well as a wide variety of storytellers and artists. *Time* magazine listed it at number twenty-nine on its list of the 100 most influential nonfiction books since the magazine was first published in 1923.

Joseph Campbell was, himself, a man of many talents and remarkable connections. He played saxophone in a jazz band well enough to support himself financially during his college days at Columbia University. He was an elite track athlete and, for a time, was among the fastest half-milers in the world. He befriended Jiddu Krishnamurti on a ship sailing for Europe, spent a year or so with Carol and John Steinbeck and the marine biologist Ed Ricketts[1] in Monterey, California, and even accompanied Ricketts on a fishing boat, collecting specimens along the Alaskan coast. In 1933, he moved into a cottage with no running water in Woodstock, NY, and for a year did little but read and write. In 1934, he began a thirty-eight-year teaching career in the literature department at Sarah Lawrence College.

People born in a particular place at a particular time may resonate so completely—in mind, body, and spirit—with the zeitgeist of their era as to become a living embodiment of that age. With such people there is also an almost chemical reaction between themselves and their culture. As much as an individual's life and work are influenced by an age, at the same time they themselves define the age. I believe Joseph Campbell was one of these people.

To understand Campbell and his work we need to understand Modernism. Modernism was an artistic and philosophical movement that arose in the late nineteenth and early twentieth centuries that prioritized individualism and symbolism. Campbell was born into a time and a culture, and near a city—New York—which were, or soon would be, awash in Modernism. Whether by temperament, osmosis, or both, so was he. With its emphasis on symbolism and interior individual experience, Modernism helped shape Campbell's thinking and writing.

Modernism was the air Campbell breathed. Campbell was born in 1904. Hannah Arendt was born two years later. George Orwell was born a year earlier than Campbell, John Steinbeck two years earlier, and Louis Armstrong—jazz music's most brilliant innovator—was only three years older. Freud's *The Interpretation of Dreams* is four years older, published in 1900, and that same year, that keg of human dynamite named Friedrich Nietzsche died. Martin Heidegger published *Being and Time* in 1927, when Campbell was twenty-three. James Joyce and Virginia Woolf were both born in 1882, only a generation before Campbell, and they both died in 1941, when Campbell was well into adulthood at the age of thirty-seven. So steeped in Modernism was he that, only two or three years after its publication, Campbell already understood the significance of, and was writing publicly about, *Finnegans Wake*. Five years after the publication of *Finnegans Wake*, he published a guide to understanding Joyce's confounding text, entitled *A Skeleton Key to Finnegans Wake*.

By the time Campbell came of age in the Roaring Twenties, Modernist architecture, art, dance, music, and literature were in full flower.

Modernism is most recognizable by its passion for the new: new forms of art, new philosophies and spiritual practices, new systems and fabrics of social order. In Modernism, traditional forms and old structures were discarded. Innovation and a searching, rigorously analytical inwardness defined the artistic values of the age. Modernism championed hard-earned experience and independent thought. Modernists sought out intellectual and sometimes even physical danger, and cultivated a self-reflective eloquence that tended toward reformulations of hidebound customs and unquestioned orthodoxies.

The *avant-garde* poet Guillaume Apollinaire (1880–1918) reached out to middle-class readers, begging them to open their minds to the new art, pleading "We want to give you vast and strange domains where mystery in flower spreads out for those who would pluck it."[2] Sergei Diaghilev, founder of Ballets Russes in 1909, told his choreographers to "Astonish me!"[3] The sculptor Claes Oldenburg (1929–2022) once remarked that what was needed was "to restore the magic inherent in the universe."[4] In his study of mythology, Joseph Campbell certainly responded to these exhortations. Take, for example, the first two of what Campbell termed the four functions of mythology:

> That's the first function of mythology, to evoke in the individual a sense of grateful, affirmative awe before the

monstrous mystery that is existence. The second function of mythology is to present an image of the cosmos, an image of the universe round about, that will maintain and elicit this experience of awe. This function we may call the cosmological function of mythology.[5]

What's more, Campbell's well-known phrase "Follow your bliss" seems comfortably at home alongside those other Modernist credos. I believe this post-Christian era added energy and depth to Campbell's thinking about mythology. By the way, post-Christian, especially in terms of Modernism, was not atheism; many new spiritual and metaphysical explorations were emerging, and some, like spiritualism, Theosophy, and Christian Science, were very popular. It was into this *milieu* that Joseph Campbell introduced a reimagined study of mythology, relating the rituals and beliefs of ancient societies to modern lives.

Joseph Campbell strikes me as having been thoroughly modern. That was the lens through which he saw the world throughout his life. After viewing the first *Star Wars* trilogy at George Lucas's Skywalker Ranch with Campbell, his friend Barbara McClintock recalls the moment the third film ended: "'It was very quiet in the dark, and Joe said, 'You know, I thought real art had stopped with Picasso, Joyce, and Mann.'"[6]

To the end of his life, the yardstick he used to measure art was Modernism.

Modernism is my favorite destination in the history of ideas—its literature, its art, and of course, its jazz. I value its striving for a deep interiority and analytical self-reflection. These qualities of Modernism were influential for Campbell, and were later

mistaken by some critics to indicate Campbell's disregard for the academic study of myth. This is a criticism of Campbell which I have never understood, because Campbell seems to have been well aware of what was going on, not just in the academic study of mythology but in anthropology, too.

Campbell was resolutely optimistic and an intellectual *bon vivant*—an engaging conversationalist, ready with a witticism, an anecdote, an easy laugh, a trenchant observation. These are the very qualities that I enjoy so much in his work. He luxuriated in the life of the mind and the adventures of travel, embracing curiosity, analytical thinking, and new intellectual discoveries, especially in literature, art, music, and dance. Campbell knew that opening the mind can expand the heart.

The Psychology of Myth

I am a depth psychologist in private practice. My clients bring issues to my office ranging from neurosis and psychopathology to personal growth and creativity. Maybe that's why I'm drawn to Campbell's impressive grasp of the concepts related to psychodynamic psychotherapies. Campbell's mastery of this subject is on full display in *Pathways to Bliss: Mythology and Personal Transformation*.

James Hillman, the founder of Archetypal Psychology, remarked that the psyche is always mythologizing.[7] And I believe the reverse of Hillman's comment is also true: that for contemporary people, myth is always psychologizing. I believe that mythic metaphors naturally lead us to find mythic correlates at work in our own inner worlds. Myths seem to constantly call into question their own authority, and they frequently reveal a rather sly cheekiness, in that while they insist that the reader take the narratives literally, they also function like a set of Rorschach cards upon which the viewer can project all sorts of subjective meanings and yet simultaneously demand a unified, collective reading.

Myths also concentrate the mind on big questions: Who am I, where do I come from, how must I live, where do I go when I die? Myth tries to understand human existence as it is consciously and unconsciously lived. The inner processes activated by myth shape the outer world, manifesting in social, political, and religious institutions, as well as the arts, creating a world view which informs scientific investigations into the nature of reality itself.

Events of the greatest historical magnitude still require an individual psychological response and boil down to an individual psychological problem. Therefore, the psychological function of mythology is no small thing, for it must carry the individual through all life's developmental stages from birth to death. The psychological function of myth helps us understand our passions, the calamities and accidents (happy or tragic) that we are heir to, and our relationships to life in the stream of time. In other words, myth can reconcile us to the conditions of life and living. We learn to live by our own lights, passions, and judgments.

This is what it means to follow our bliss, and also why it's so difficult. It's dangerous to confront the edges of ourselves, or the necessity of changing our lives.[8] But we must be willing to transgress those limits—both internal and external. Mythic and metaphorical thinking is an essential part of that project.

Mythic thinking *is* the activity of working at the limits of oneself. It is there, at the edges of the self, that myth helps us discover new narratives for our own lives. Ludwig Wittgenstein insisted that the limits of our language, our thinking, define the limits of our world.[9] What I do as a psychotherapist is just that: I try to help people discover a new narrative, or new images, with which to explore, reconfigure, and expand the limits of their worlds. That's why Joseph Campbell once remarked to Bill Moyers that if you have a myth you don't need psychotherapy.

The choice to follow one's bliss is a radical, risky, psychological move. It is a commitment to live authentically, to be as honest as we can be, forsaking the lies we tell ourselves about ourselves and the world, and to work to accept the world exactly as it is. Such authenticity and radical acceptance free us from struggling against life and let us choose our attitude regardless of our circumstances. Then we discover what we are truly capable of becoming, and recognize that life is beautiful, even when it seems sad or tragic.

In *Pathways to Bliss*, Joseph Campbell uses the theories of depth psychology, particularly those of C.G. Jung and Sigmund Freud, to unpack the psychologizing function of myth:

> The myth must carry the individual through the stages of his life, from birth through maturity through senility to death. The mythology must do so in accord with the social order of his group, the cosmos as understood by his group, and the monstrous mystery.[10]

By introducing the notion of being in "accord with the social order of a group" (we could substitute the word *culture* for *group*),

Campbell is referring to a functional, living mythology, something contemporary life seems to lack, at least at the level of society and culture. And, deprived of the rituals of a living mythology, "the outer world fails to invoke," Campbell says, our "psychological participation, [and] you turn inward."[11] The inward turn is a response to an external mythlessness, and consists of first discovering, and then working with, the inner world of images and imagination, sensation, thought, and emotion. From there, one begins to discover one's own singular destiny, how might it be fulfilled, and what unique gifts one can offer the world.

The Greek word *therapeia* refers to healing, curing, treating, but it also means to perform a service, a waiting on. From that perspective, an inward turn involves a kind of psychological hosting; paying deep attention to and getting to know one's inner world—the good and bad, the terrifying and comforting, who we desire to be and who we are. This therapeutic hosting is like the service at a restaurant. The food is nourishing and delicious, the waiter never interrupts, water glasses are always full, bread is always present and warm, and there is no sense of urgency, no anxiety that you shouldn't take the time to enjoy the experience.

If one approaches the soul with the same accommodating, welcoming manner—the attitude of *therapeia*—one discovers within oneself the equally satisfying and memorable experience of self-awareness and self-acceptance, a confidence that allows one to inhabit the world more authentically while simultaneously giving to it the gift of oneself.

Chapters and Themes

Pathways to Bliss: Mythology and Personal Transformation was created from a dozen or more interviews, lectures, and seminars that Joseph Campbell gave between 1962 and 1983. The book consists of seven chapters, the final chapter being a transcription of questions and answers that range widely over topics explored in the various chapters.

In the introduction to *Pathways to Bliss,* Campbell introduces the idea that mythology plays an important role in the psychological life of the individual. He quotes the German psychiatrist Karlfried Graf Dürckheim, who argued that a "life wisdom" lives in each of us, and that "We are all manifestations of a mystic power: the power of life, which has shaped all life, and which has shaped us all in our mother's womb."[12] From Dürckheim, Campbell borrows the phrase "transparent to the transcendent," an important phrase that the reader will encounter several times in this book, which refers to a way of working with the metaphors of myth so that that the self-consciousness of thinking and speaking in metaphor drops away and the transcendent reality to which the myths are pointing becomes an organic, individual reality relevant to one's individual life right here, right now.

Chapters I (*The Necessity of Rites*) and II (*Myth Through Time*) explore the use of ritual and myth to help individuals reconcile themselves to the conditions of life, conditions that sometimes seem to stand against life itself. We are introduced to Campbell's four functions of mythology, with particular emphasis on the first and fourth functions: The first function of myth is to evoke a sense of awe in respect to the unfathomable mystery of existence, while the fourth function of myth—and main focus of this text—is to place the individual in accord with their own development as a human being, and the unique challenges of living a human life. Campbell also gives a concise summary of the history and development of myth through time and its migration around the world.

Chapters III (*Society and Symbol*), IV (*Myth and the Self*), and V (*Personal Myth*) focus on the sociology and psychology of myth, the way myths influence cultures, and more specifically, how myth influences individuals and individual psychology. Campbell relies on Freudian and Jungian theories of psychology to explore the fourth function of mythology, what he calls the pedagogical and psychological function. Jung's notion of archetypes such as the Shadow and the Anima, and the theory of psychological types such as Introversion and Extroversion, are especially relevant to Campbell's explanation of the psychological impact and the orienting power of myths. Finally, Campbell explores the value of myth for individuals who live in a largely secular, mythless time.

Chapter VI (*The Self as Hero*) is a review of the phenomenally popular idea of the hero's adventure, which Campbell introduced in his classic work *The Hero with a Thousand Faces*. The hero's journey is a persistent idea, an archetypal motif (James Joyce called it the monomyth), that appears not just in myth and literature: If one is attentive, it may even reveal the significant movements—the plot, if you will—of one's own life. Campbell remarks at the end of Chapter VI

> What I think is that a good life is one hero journey after another. Over and over again, you are called to new horizons ... the dangers are there, the help also, and the

fulfillment or the fiasco. There's always the possibility of a fiasco.

But there's also the possibility of bliss.[13]

Chapter VII is a transcript of discussions Campbell has with his audience, those who attended the lectures from which this volume is composed. This chapter presents an opportunity to clarify issues from the lecture or seek answers to questions that the reader may hold in common with Campbell's audience, such as an explanation of the power of the mythic image and its role in our lives, and aspects of Jungian psychological theory and application. Finally, there is a discussion regarding the archetypal feminine, the role of women in mythology, and the particular relevance myth has to the lives of women.

Conclusion

In *Pathways to Bliss*, you will find references to "personal mythology" scattered throughout the text. Personal mythology means something quite different to Joseph Campbell than how the term is often understood in popular culture or in New Age spirituality. Too often, myth is entertained as a parlor game whose only object is that of identifying one's ego with the patterns of a particular archetype, while simultaneously neglecting the frequently perilous challenges of archetypal realities.

Personalizing myth and its archetypal images in this manner is similar to a butterfly collector pinning a butterfly in a shadow box: The object of beauty and fascination, the object of a particular kind of awe, is no longer alive. Likewise, a mythic image is

reduced to a psychic tchotchke, an amusing object, in which one is no longer able to find sentient beauty or follow its unhurried, meandering way that almost always leads into the unfamiliar territory of one's own psyche and the sublime discoveries awaiting one there.

Thinking about a personal relationship to myth and focusing on what the mythological metaphors are suggesting—what the metaphors point toward—is where one finds the real power of myth. Thus employed, myth can diminish the influence of the self-aggrandizing ego. "So this wisdom that comes through [a particular individual] comes from the ages; it has nothing to do with this moment here and now, nor with the person who is transmitting it."[14] Mythic images then become more than mere stories; they provide the means to identify, not with the myth, but with what the myth points to: the transcendent cosmic force that begets life itself.

NOTES

1 Ed Ricketts was an important figure in the lives of both John Steinbeck and Joseph Campbell. Steinbeck based the character of Doc in his novel *Cannery Row* on Ricketts, and Campbell once remarked that, "It was Ed who was especially important to me, because he reinforced the interest in biology that I had had as a prep school student. And from our long talks about biology, I eventually came up with one of my basic viewpoints: that myth is a function of biology [...] In other words, myth is as fundamental to us as our capacity to speak and think and dream." (Highwater, Jamake. "A Conversation with Joseph Campbell." *Inward*, C.G. Jung Foundation, 1985).

2 Peter Gay, *Modernism: The Lure of Heresy: From Baudelaire to Beckett and Beyond* (2008), 16.
3 Ibid, 3.
4 Ibid, 7.
5 Joseph Campbell, *Pathways to Bliss*, 6–7.
6 Stephen Larsen and Robin Larsen, *Joseph Campbell: A Fire in the Mind: The Authorized Biography* (Inner Traditions, 2002), 691.
7 James Hillman, *In Defense of Jung* seminar, March 18–19, 2005, Santa Barbara, CA.
8 W.H. Auden captured this fact of life perfectly in his poem "Leap Before You Look," which begins with this stanza:

> The sense of danger must not disappear:
> The way is certainly both short and steep,
> However gradual it looks from here;
> Look if you like but you will have to leap.

9 I want to again point out the revolutionary impact of Modernism. Wittgenstein wrote his notes for the *Tractatus* while he was a soldier during WWI, and finished the book while on leave in 1918. The horrors of The Great War no doubt reinforced, and even intensified, Modernism's desire for the new and its self-conscious desire to refashion and revitalize a world that many saw as bloody, corrupt, and morally bankrupt.
10 Campbell, *Pathways to Bliss*, 9.
11 Ibid, 100.
12 Ibid, xvi.
13 Ibid, 133.
14 Ibid, 59.

Chapter I
The Necessity of Rites

Chapter Summary

In the first chapter of *Pathways to Bliss*, Joseph Campbell addresses why myth matters, and introduces his four functions of mythology. These four functions describe how a working, living mythology orients individuals to the conditions of life, and explains the universe in a way that is consistent with contemporary observations of it. Functional mythologies organize societies, and explain the individual to itself—practically, intellectually, and spiritually.

Next, Campbell discusses myth and the development of the individual. In this section, he speaks to the psychological development that all human beings experience and some challenges we all face: the dependency that forms the first stage of our development, later attempts to become more independent from parents and caretakers, the transformation from childhood to adulthood with its greater demands and responsibilities, and finally, figuring out the role that one plays within the context of family, work, and the traditions of one's culture. He discusses how roles in society evolve as we age, and illustrates how, as we move into the final years of life, myth may help us prepare for what he calls the "journey out the dark door"[1]—that journey the poet Phillip Larkin called "the supine stationary voyage."[2]

Finally, Campbell addresses myths for the future. The present day seems to be mythless, a time of "broken symbols," as Campbell puts it, in which mythic narratives simply can't be taken as literally as they once were. The old mythological traditions are no longer authoritative sources for understanding the world, what's in it, and how it came to be. Today, mythic narratives and symbols no longer emanate from divine authority, and science refutes the traditions and images of myth. The value of myths, Campbell says, is found in viewing them as metaphors that put one in touch with the transcendent source of the mystery that is life, the fundamental ground of existence. There is a formula for living a richly satisfying life, a saying to which Campbell repeatedly returns in *Pathways to Bliss*, namely becoming "transparent to the transcendent," which we will unpack later in this study guide. It is a phrase that describes a psychological move that unites the inner and outer worlds and provides a way forward towards potential mythologies of the future. But first, he says, we must move "past the broken symbols of the present and begin to forge new working images, images that are *transparent to the transcendent*."[3]

For the development of these "new working images," perhaps we may find that artists and poets are creating new images—narratives and symbols—that may eventually lead to new mythologies that are relevant to contemporary life and a modern scientific understanding of the world, which also offer deeply felt meaning to the human beings who inhabit future ages.

THE FUNCTIONS OF MYTHOLOGY

The first function of mythology, Campbell says, "is to reconcile consciousness to the preconditions of its own existence; that is to say, to the nature of life."[4] In other words, life is hard. Life lives on other life, and sometimes you're the diner and sometimes you're

"A mythological order is a system of images that gives consciousness a sense of meaning in existence, which, my dear friend, has no meaning—it simply is."

—PATHWAYS TO BLISS, *page 6*

the dinner, metaphorically and literally. But the conditions of life were established billions of years before there was a human being present to witness them. The world has no need to reconcile itself to us, but rather we must find a way to reconcile ourselves to the world and to life as it presents itself to us. Such a reconciliation is the first function of mythology: to make one aware that life as it is, with all its pain, with all its horror, isn't just a festival of suffering. Life may be lived with love and with gratitude, recognizing the sweetness and the wonder that it also contains.

Campbell theorizes that there may not be any mythology before the eighth century BCE that was world-negating, meaning that it refused the conditions of life. Paleolithic and early Neolithic mythologies appeared to have affirmed life to its core, even though their rituals graphically reflected the horrors of life.

So, Campbell's first function of mythology is to find a way to radically accept and affirm the conditions of life exactly as they are without needing life to be different in any way. Alternatively, one might reject the world as it is and not participate in it at all. At that point, one's sole aim is to find a way out of the world. A third perspective is activism, in which one will only affirm the world once they make it the way they want it to be.

The second function of mythology, Campbell continues, is cosmological, to provide an image of the universe that fills the individual with a sense of awe. Ideally, such an idea or image would incorporate what we know to be true in terms of the discernable, factual universe, because the cosmological function of mythology serves not only to instill in us a sense of awe, but to give us a kind of practical, informative understanding of how the universe works.

Campbell's third function of mythology is sociological: upholding the laws and customs on which a society is based.[5] Generally speaking, there are no avenues, procedures, or appeals open to one that might amend or mitigate these laws or rules—one cannot simply decide this law or that rule is out of date, illogical, or even irrational; if you happen to live in the social unit to which these laws apply, they give you no option but to obey. The socially ordering rules and laws of mythology are like the laws of the universe, and you disobey them at your own considerable risk.

It is important to understand that the second and third functions of mythology are, in modern life, covered by other domains. Today cosmology is better understood through astronomy, astrophysics, and exogeology (also known as astrogeology). Around 3,600 years ago, the earth was thought to be a flat disk floating on a cosmic sea; by around 2,500 years ago the Greeks concluded that the earth was in fact spherical, and not flat at all.[6] Democritus offered an atomic theory of the universe, and presaging the Many Worlds Interpretation (MWI) of quantum mechanics, Anaximander postulated the existence of multiple, or perhaps even an infinite number, of universes. Less than 500 years ago, Nicholas Copernicus published his treatise *De Revolutionibus Orbium Coelestium*, in which he provides evidence for a heliocentric universe. In the sciences, knowledge is always engaged in the process of innovation, augmentation, correction, or refutation, whereas in mythology it seems that, as Campbell put it, "the older the doctrine, the truer it is held to be."[7]

Regarding the sociological function of mythology, most people no longer believe that laws or behavioral norms and rules are inspired by a god or gods; nor do we believe that they are handed down to us by some divine decree or holy fiat. Laws are created by a particular society and its people, for their particular time. Laws can be modified and even repealed entirely, and generally speaking, they pertain to contemporary issues regarding living in a given city, state, or country.

Where that leaves us, then, is with the first function of mythology, which I've described above, and Campbell's fourth function of mythology, which is a psychological function. Sometimes Campbell refers to this function as pedagogical, which means having a teaching or educational function. The psychological function relates to how a curious, learning, evolving, reasonably self-aware person tries to make sense of life in an always-changing world.

MYTH AND THE DEVELOPMENT OF THE INDIVIDUAL

The psychological function of mythology helps the individual understand and move through the various stages of development throughout the course of a human life. The main concerns of the fourth function are found first in bringing a child from abject dependence through to maturity and relative independence, and later helping the elderly disengage from an active life of skill and expertise, withdraw from their responsibilities, and transition into retirement. The psychological function of myth also facilitates the ultimate transition out of this life and into "that undiscovered country" of death.

MYTHS FOR THE FUTURE

This is an area of mythology that is very difficult to address. The difficulty of trying to imagine what myths will emerge in the future arises out of three persistent facts. The first fact is that it takes a very, very long time to make a myth. So long, in fact, that one can have no idea of what life might be like for human beings, what issues might be of the utmost concern or importance that far into the future. Circumstances can change rapidly; societies rise and decline; climate change, food insecurities, nation-state conflict can all foster symbolic images and narratives that capture the human imagination, and be incorporated into what may eventually become myth.

The second fact is that myths are spontaneous creations of the *unconscious* mind. In other words, myths cannot be intentionally created. The formation of a myth is indisputably tied to the interplay of creative minds, which is why Campbell often referred to artists and poets as the mythmakers of the future. Myth won't emerge from science because, going forward, science will always seem to be at odds with myth. Yet, science won't replace myth, either, because the issue isn't simply that the gods and goddesses are myths, rather that myths are the disclosure of the transcendent mysteries of human existence. So, it's not just any art that may become myth, it's specifically the kind of art or literature that allows the transcendent phenomena to shine through.

The third fact is that myths are always related to a particular group of people, in a particular place, at a particular time. At present, the world is truly a global community with interdependent economies, political systems, and cultural influences. Information and communication are instantaneous around the world, and relationships are no longer confined to specific geographic areas. We are in many ways a global village, and whatever myths are to arise in the future will, I believe, be grounded in that reality.

"We need mythology as the marsupial needs the pouch to develop beyond the stage of the incompetent infant to a stage where it can step out of the pouch and say, 'Me, voilà: I'm it.'"

—PATHWAYS TO BLISS, *page 18*

Chapter I: The Necessity of Rites

Points of Interest

THE ETERNAL DIMENSION OF THE SELF

Perhaps one of the more emphatic points Campbell makes in *Pathways to Bliss* is that it is a mistake to think that some sort of eternity awaits us when we die. In Campbell's thought, eternity is right here and right now, and if you "Find that eternal dimension in yourself … you will ride through time and throughout the whole length of your days."[8] In other words, there is a dimension of a human being (the deathless soul, if you will) that transcends personal, historical, and physical experiences. The images and narratives of mythology support investigations into that dimension.

CAMPBELL'S MODERNISM

I mentioned in the introduction that if one wants to understand Campbell, one must be aware of Modernism. At the end of Chapter I we find Campbell returning to his Modernist wellspring, referring to Thomas Mann and James Joyce, artists whom he held in the highest esteem because of their ability to take Medieval mythic themes and spin them into modern artistic gold, writing:

> … Stephen and Hans [Stephen Dedalus and Hans Castorp, perhaps the best-known characters created by Joyce and Mann, respectively] are *in the modern culture field* (my emphasis). They're having experiences relevant to the conflicts and problems that you're experiencing, and they are consequently models for you to recognize your own experience.[9]

"People live by playing a game, and you can ruin a game by being Sir Sobersides who comes in and says, 'Well, what's the use of this?' A cosmological image gives you a field in which to play the game that helps you to reconcile your life, your existence, to your own consciousness, or expectation, of meaning."

—PATHWAYS TO BLISS, *page 7*

Chapter I: The Necessity of Rites

Campbell has, in his various lectures, essays, and books, often remarked on the uncanny parallels between James Joyce and Thomas Mann; how Joyce in his Catholicism follows Dante, and Mann in his Protestantism follows Goethe. Campbell, too, carries on Ezra Pound's Modernist credo "Make it new!" in bringing not just Medieval, but also Paleolithic myths into the modern culture field, and into our own lives. However, Modernism is not simply about making new ideas and images. Modernism has a beautiful formality, but it's an easy, stylish (dare I say democratic?) formality, denuded of the sometimes-stuffy formal beauty of Realism, or the resplendent histrionics of Romanticism. Hmm. Just like Joseph Campbell, himself.

Complementary Reading from Campbell's Work

Campbell, Joseph. *The Inner Reaches of Outer Space: Metaphor as Myth and as Religion.* New World Library, 2012.

—. *The Masks of God, Vol. 4: Creative Mythology.* Penguin, 1968.

Campbell, Joseph, and Bradley Olson. "The Impact of Science on Myth." *Pathways with Joseph Campbell,* season 1, episode 10. Joseph Campbell Foundation MythMaker Podcast Network.

Further Reading

Gay, Peter. *Modernism: The Lure of Heresy.* W.W. Norton & Company, 2010.

Mann, Thomas. *The Magic Mountain.* Vintage, 1996.

Turner, Victor. *The Ritual Process: Structure and Anti-Structure.* Routledge, 2017.

Discussion Questions

- Name and briefly discuss the four functions of mythology as Joseph Campbell has identified them in Chapter I of this book. Which function seems most important to you, and why? Which seems least important, and why?

- Campbell suggests that myth no longer fulfills its the second and third functions. Do you agree or disagree, and why?

- In what ways do people develop in the same ways across cultures and traditions? How do people develop differently in various cultures and traditions?

Essay Topics

- Describe the ways in which myth impacts the development of the individual.

- How might outdated mythological traditions negatively impact contemporary life? Choose one example and write an essay exploring those impacts.

- Write a paper comparing and contrasting mythology and psychology. Where do you see their similarities, differences, and areas of overlap?

Chapter I: The Necessity of Rites

Creative Prompts

- Design two complementary rituals: one to help people through the experience of starting school, and another to help people through the experience of finishing school. Think about how your rituals could honor where the person is right now, and prepare them for the changes they are about to experience.

- Write a story that you wish someone had told you to help you through a difficult time in your life.

- Write in your journal about stories that have impacted your development at key points in your life. How can you imagine stories impacting your life in the future?

NOTES

1 Joseph Campbell, *Pathways to Bliss*, 17.
2 Phillip Larkin, "An Arundel Tomb," *Phillip Larkin Poems: Selected by Martin Amis*, Faber and Faber Ltd., London, 2011.
3 Campbell, *Pathways to Bliss*, 20 (emphasis mine).
4 Ibid, 3.
5 Ibid, 8.
6 Remarkably, there is a small but fiercely committed group who still insist the earth is flat, known as the Flat Earth Society. Somewhere, Eratosthenes (who, 2,200 years ago, estimated the circumference of the earth to within a mere 500 miles) is rolling his eyes.
7 Campbell, *Pathways to Bliss*, 9.
8 Ibid, 18.
9 Ibid, 20.

Chapter II
Myth Through Time

Chapter Summary

In Chapter II, Joseph Campbell addresses foundational themes that are crucial to understanding mythology. He begins by explaining "The Surface and Substance of Myth." This section is fundamental to understanding how Campbell thinks about myth, where mythology comes from, and how it informs cultures around the world. He also prepares us for a deeper discussion, in Chapter IV, of the psychology of C.G. Jung and the concept of archetypes. Here he reinforces the importance of the fourth function of mythology, the psychological function.

In the section "The Birth of Myth: Primitive and Early Societies," Campbell examines the way that mythology transformed during "the three great periods of the human race."[1] These periods encompass the eons of time from the birth of human consciousness, across the vast expanse of history, and into the modern age. He describes how cultures, and by extension their mythologies, are influenced by their environs: the weather and climate, the surrounding terrain (mountains, plains, forests, etc.), flora (grasses, trees, etc.), the fertility of the soil, and the wildlife present in the area. Campbell also gives examples of rituals associated with particular mythological systems and the way in which ritual makes a reality of the world view articulated in the myth.

Finally, Campbell examines "The Birth of East and West: The High Cultures." In this section, Campbell explores theories that account for the differences between traditional mythological world

"One might reasonably define mythology as other people's religion. The definition of religion is equally uncomplicated: it is misunderstood mythology. The misunderstanding consists typically in interpreting mythological symbols as though they were references to historical facts."

—PATHWAYS TO BLISS, *page 21*

views of Asia and Europe. He notes, of course, that mythologies and world views on different continents are not monolithic, and vary depending on regional and cultural traditions. But he does offer criticism of the tendency of monotheistic religions to have a supreme—and sometimes supremely angry—male deity, which in many ways seems counterintuitive to our experience of Nature.

In traditions that derive from Europe, we are in a *relationship* to a masculine God, there is *distance* between humans and their deity, a sense of powerlessness, and in some cases, *alienation*. But in Asian nations such as China and India, deities transcend gender, and rather than trying to create a special relationship with God, the spiritual goal is to recognize that we are each the mask, or manifestation, of the deity. The difference between Asia and Europe is not so much in the symbolism or metaphors of their mythologies, but rather how those metaphors and symbols are understood, interpreted, and taught. More important is what we do with these symbols. What matters, for Campbell, is your relationship to the symbol, and being able to find in the myth "the birth of the mystic, mythic being that is your own spiritual life."[2]

THE SURFACE AND SUBSTANCE OF MYTH

In Campbell's view, the same basic themes of mythology exist all around the world. Problems begin when we literalize the images and narratives of myth and insist on understanding them as history. Then one group accuses another of being wrong, because their own system is obviously the only "correct" one. That's why Campbell says that myth is "other people's religion."[3]

There is a strong temptation to see myth and religion as a set of historical facts, their narratives literally true, and their characters as real as you and I. For many people, the insistence upon the literal truth of mythic narratives has the unintended consequence of destroying their belief in and awe before the symbol, when they reject the symbol as untrue. This is truly unfortunate because the literal, historical aspects of mythology are insignificant compared to what these stories reveal about our deepest, shared human nature, and our fears, desires, passions, and imagination. These symbols emerge from the human psyche, they link us to the depths of our being, and communicate to us the richness and the vitality of those depths, which are in turn linked to the mysterious, often immaterial realities of the world itself, and to the energies of life.

Campbell touches upon the notion of the "elementary idea," *das Elementargedanke*, a term introduced by Adolf Bastian. Bastian was a nineteenth century German intellectual who took note of what he saw as the universal nature of symbols. Campbell points out that symbols are expressed in different ways in different cultures (what Bastian called *Volkergedanke*, or folk ideas, which are related to a specific culture with a common language, customs, and ideals), and they still might have similar meanings. For instance, a wolf and a shark symbolize the same toothy, primal, consuming fear even though one inhabits a forest and the other the deep blue sea. As Campbell points out, whether you're watching *Hamlet* performed by Chinese actors in Hong Kong or by Jewish actors in New York City—or even, I would add, performed in contemporary clothing and set in a modern city—it is still the same play that Shakespeare wrote around the year 1600 CE.

In the last pages of this section, Campbell returns to the notion that ever-evolving scientific knowledge, and revolutionary changes to social structures have made the cosmological and social functions of mythology less relevant today. What remains unchanged, however, are "the basic psychological problems of youth, maturity, old age, and death—and the mystical problem of the universe."[4] In other words, functions one and four remain viable, and it is in these domains that we might repurpose or rehabilitate mythological traditions, separating them from their ancient cosmology and social theory, and using them to explore the depths and mysteries of our own psyche and life, and of the world.

THE BIRTH OF MYTH: PRIMITIVE AND EARLY SOCIETIES

Campbell notes three great periods in human history: the primitive period, the great middle period, and the modern period. The primitive period begins with the Paleolithic era and runs through the Neolithic era to about 5,500 years ago, when writing was invented in Mesopotamia. Interestingly, more recent scholarship tells us that writing was independently invented in China around 3,200 years ago, and in the lowland areas of what is now Mexico and Guatemala around 2,500 years ago. The great middle period, which began around 3,500 BCE, gave rise to revolutionary technologies like writing, the wheel, and the plough. City-states and kingships began to emerge during the early stages of this time period. And finally, the modern period begins with the European Renaissance and refinements to scientific methodology, the beginning of mechanization and machinery, and a more secular and humanist world view.

This section focuses on "primitive and early societies," and here Campbell finds two primary attitudes. The first, relating

"The next point, however, is that this power, which transcends all thought, is the very essence of your own being. It is immanent—it is right here, right now, here in the paper of this book, in the chair you're sitting in."

—PATHWAYS TO BLISS, *page 40*

to hunting cultures of the Paleolithic and Neolithic eras, is the idea that *"there is no such thing as death."*[5] This idea arises from the fact that these early peoples lived in a world of killing and bloodshed, so they had to figure out a way to protect themselves from the emotional and psychological toll of all this killing.

One way to create a psychological defense to killing is to regard the act of killing as sacred, and to regard the animal as a willing victim, sacrificing itself for the good of all. Humans survived not just on the meat of the killed animal, but on every other part as well: bones became tools, skin became clothing and shelter, and so forth. In return, rituals were performed for the animals to let them know they were honored and respected, and that the people were grateful, all in the hope that the animal would return to life so the cycle could begin all over again. This attitude is neatly captured in the Latin phrase *mors tua, vita mea*: "your death, my life." Because the act of killing was sacred, the relationship between the killed and the killer was also sacred, and there would be no waste, no indiscriminate killing, and never more animals killed than were needed for survival. This illustrates what we would describe today as an ecological sensibility toward the natural world based on the idea of conservation.

But something else was happening as well. All this killing led Paleolithic hunters to atone for the separation of humans from the rest of nature through the human sacrifice. These ritual killings were considered sacred, and they became vital, necessary atonements, or *at-one*-ments, which restored balance and consecrated the cycles of living and dying as generative and creative, rather than destructive. These rituals grounded participants in a mythological reality in which life and death were mutually dependent upon one another, and honored rather than dreaded.

Chapter II: Myth Through Time

The second notable attitude of this period comes later, perhaps around the time of the development of agriculture, when some cultures began to see the earth and all living things as in service to human beings. In this view, the earth itself and her products are simply resources that may be used and discarded, with no regard for ecological principles or relationships between humans and the natural world. "That's a ruthless attitude," Campbell concludes.[6]

After relating a Blackfoot myth on the origins of the Buffalo Dance, Campbell pivots to the tropical world where we find an entirely different mythology shaped, as mythologies frequently are, by a very different geography. Here Campbell introduces the word *paideumatic*, which simply means that cultures are shaped by their physical settings. Myths in tropical settings portray a fecund earth, watery and lush, luxuriant with vegetation and biodiversity,[7] and here, unlike hunting cultures in less hospitable climates, women are the symbolic representation of the earth and its creative, generative powers.

These tropical regions introduce—at least from our contemporary perspective—horrifying rituals of human sacrifice. Living in a rainforest, one sees decaying vegetation all around, and from these heaps of decay new life grows. Campbell remarks, "The obvious lesson emerges: out of death comes life … and if you want to increase life, then you must increase death!"[8] Consequently, mythologies evolve that sanctify human sacrifice.

The basic myth of these cultures, Campbell says, is that there was a time when there was no time, a mythological age in which beings were neither human nor animal nor plant. There was no death or birth, and this age ends with what Campbell calls elsewhere the "Mythological Event," which is the murder of one of

45

"And so we come to this point: anything that you can name is not it. That which you can name in yourself, you are not it, and yet you are it; that self-contradictory statement gives us the key to the mystery of what we call the Mystery of the East."

—PATHWAYS TO BLISS, *page 40*

these beings. Its body is cut up and buried (planted), and out of the buried pieces grow the food plants people depend upon. What you're eating, what supports you, is your relative, your ancestor, someone very close to you, something of which you were once a part until the psychological development of individuality in human beings emerges.

The rituals belonging to this tradition are reenactments of the primal murder, the burial of the victim's parts, and the subsequent growth of the life-sustaining food. These rituals resulted in, to our modern sensibility, horrifying acts of group homicide. But no individual or cultural guilt was experienced because these rituals facilitated an implicit return to the mythic age, an age which was not located in some distant, murky, past, but embedded right here and now in the present by means of the ritual.

The rituals discussed in this section all point to the fundamental—one might even say elementary—idea that life is a cyclical phenomenon that constantly appears, vanishes, and returns. We are powerless to interrupt it, so these rituals attempt to place these cultures in harmony with the cyclical, recurring nature of existence.

THE BIRTH OF EAST AND WEST: THE HIGH CULTURES

Campbell divides what he calls the "high cultures"[9] into two large geographic areas: Asia (the Orient, or the East) and Europe (the Occident, or the West). The line dividing East and West passes, Campbell says, through Persia. East of Persia are two main centers: India and the Far East, which includes Japan, China, and Southeast Asia. West of Persia are also two main centers of culture: the Near East and Europe.

In contrast to East Asia, which was relatively isolated, the Near East and Europe were often besieged by warrior peoples—Aryans from the north and Semitic peoples from the south. After the warrior cultures gained control, they ruled over farmers, artisans, and merchants whose mytho-religious life was determined by priests who watched the skies for planetary movements and the passing of the seasons.

The warrior groups brought with them mythologies of masculine gods with thunderbolts at their disposal, while the land-based agriculturalists worshipped the earth as the great Mother Goddess. The conflict between these two mythological worldviews is, Campbell says, a central motif in Occidental mythology. And in the conflict between a patriarchal, uncultured, brutal warrior group and a sophisticated, urbane, goddess-worshiping culture, the brawlers prevailed, and assimilated, to some degree, the local myths. So, for example, rather than a woman, Eve, giving birth to the human race, Adam, incredibly, gives birth instead. To drive this point home, Campbell points out that in Hebrew, *adam* means "earth." The myths that once related to a great goddess have been altered to suit a masculine deity.

Campbell points out that east of Persia, in the Orient, this problem doesn't exist; the old Eastern cosmologies of cycles and an impersonal order that transcends gender and human petitions still operate today. What's more, the divine power informing the material world is "the very essence of your own being."[10] This is a key idea in the work of Joseph Campbell: *tat tvam asi*: "Thou art that." You are it, you already are the thing you're seeking. However, the you that is it is not the you of your ego, not the individual that you think you are; rather, the you that "is it" is the ineffable mystery of existence from which "you" are projected.

This is very different from a Western standpoint where the divinity—the creator—is decidedly different from the created being. The mythologies of the East say that the creator and the created are one and the same. The Western division between creator and created is responsible for the familiar sense of alienation from the divine. One consequence of that alienation is a more institutionalized relationship with the deity where an intermediary must negotiate a "personal relationship" to the divine, lest God be offended and exclude us from His divine presence.

Points of Interest

MYTHS OF SEPARATE CONSCIOUSNESS

What Campbell is pointing out in his discussion of early tropical mythologies, and I don't think this can be overstated, is that when the understanding of a human being as simply another being among the vast untold number of beings—a generous, harmonizing principle where each being is no more important than any other, and experiences no separation from the natural world at all—is betrayed, then death and hunger enter the world. I see this motif as a metaphor for the development of the subjective quality of human consciousness that separates one from everyone and everything else. Because food emerges from death, what you're eating—what supports you—is your relative, your ancestor, a being to whom you were related until the psychological development of individuality emerged.

Chapter II: Myth Through Time

LISTENING TO OTHERS' MYTHS

Campbell ends this chapter with what I believe may be understood as a bit of cautionary advice. One shouldn't casually adopt another tradition as one's own and expect it to do the heavy spiritual lifting. One must work with oneself to be capable of experiencing the symbols and metaphors of the spiritual message by making oneself "transparent to the transcendent." That is, in itself, a difficult process. It might be tempting to believe that the world and its myths are here for my personal benefit, or a sense of superiority in believing that I have found the truth that so many others have failed to apprehend. Such a stance is not personal mythology; it's personalized mythology, and rather than enabling us to reconcile ourselves to the conditions of life, it creates an ego-satisfying self-delusion and greater disharmony. I'll have more to say about this issue in Chapter V, in which Campbell discusses personal myth.

Complementary Reading from Campbell's Work

Campbell, Joseph. *Masks of God, Volume 1: Primitive Mythology.* New World Library, 2020.

—. *The Mythic Dimension: Selected Essays 1959–1987.* New World Library, 2017.

Chapter II: Myth Through Time

Further Reading

Girard, René. *The Scapegoat.* Johns Hopkins University Press, 1996.

Witzel, Michael. *The Origins of the World's Mythologies.* Oxford University Press, 2013.

Discussion Questions

- How and why do the cosmological and sociological functions of mythology no longer apply to contemporary society? Where and how do you learn about the universe and the rules of society?

- Define the word *paideumatic* and give some examples of the ways paideumatic forces may influence cultures.

- How might the rituals of myth reinforce the world views of the group? How might rituals be used to change a culture's views?

Essay Topics

- Compare and contrast how the individual is understood between Asian and European religious traditions.

- What are the differences and similarities in the attitudes of hunting and planting cultures toward death? What could each approach learn from the other?

- Explore some of the explanations for why some cultures develop monotheistic religious traditions instead of polytheistic traditions.

Creative Prompts

- Pick your favorite work of art (a song, painting, play, novel, poem, movie, or anything else) from at least fifty years ago—or more!—and create a contemporary interpretation or adaptation of it.

- Write a story in which one or more characters travel in time—to the past *and* the future—and witness myths and rituals that are very different from their own.

- Write, paint, or sculpt a scene depicting the joining of two mythic systems in a way that enriches both of them.

NOTES

1 Joseph Campbell, *Pathways to Bliss*, 26.
2 Ibid, 43.
3 Ibid, 21.
4 Ibid, 25.
5 Ibid, 27, emphasis original.
6 Ibid, 27.
7 From plants found exclusively in tropical rainforests we derive many indispensable drugs in common use throughout

the world: quinine to treat malaria, cortisone, glaucoma drugs, drugs that treat Parkinson's, and medications for multiple sclerosis, leukemia, and Hodgkin's disease.
8 Campbell, *Pathways to Bliss*, 30.
9 Ibid, 36.
10 Ibid, 40.

Chapter III
Society and Symbol

Chapter Summary

In this relatively short chapter, Joseph Campbell describes how symbols and myth act on the individual, as well as on the collective psyche.

In the first section, "The Mechanism of Myths: How Symbols Work," Campbell relates a theory regarding Innate Releasing Mechanisms, or IRMs. An IRM functions like a button which, when pressed or activated, releases and channels physical and psychic energy. IRMs are conceptually similar to C.G. Jung's notion of archetypes, affecting consciousness in a comparable way. Contemporary biology calls them Fixed Action Patterns, or FAPs. The subject of IRMs is a contentious one in contemporary biology and philosophy, so I will attempt to unpack the current debate.

In the second section, "Society, Myth, and Personal Development," Campbell takes us on a brief survey of psychoanalytic developmental theory. His synopsis is remarkably lucid and accessible given the complexity of Freudian thought regarding human development from birth through adolescence to maturity, independence, and social responsibility. In general, I believe Freud is very good when it comes to the psychodynamics of the first half of life, and Jung is an invaluable resource for the second half of life.

Finally, in "The Ego: East and West," Campbell continues his examination of the Freudian psyche by looking at the structure of the ego and the unconscious. Campbell contrasts the ego as it has developed in the Western world with the ego in the East, and explains how variations regarding the notion of a self arise. For instance, the ego construction of people in the Western world inclines them to understand God in the context of a relationship, but they are distressingly limited in their ability to "know" God. In the East, the revelation is that each person *is* God. The energies, forces, and organizing principles of life that we imagine as gods are the same energies, forces, and principles that constitute us.

There are, however, areas of overlap between the East and the West, such as the correspondences between Buddhism and depth psychology. Buddhism can be understood as an effective psychology, concerned as it is with the inner life, particularly the often-perplexing dynamics of mental life. Dialectical Behavioral Therapy (DBT) is an effective cognitive-behavioral therapeutic technique, and is deeply influenced by the Theravada Buddhist concept of "The Middle Way," incorporating meditation and mindfulness practices. DBT is particularly powerful in the treatment of borderline personality disorder, in which people tend to oscillate between emotional extremes in their relationships with others.

Both Buddhism and psychoanalysis use self-exploration and self-understanding to identify the causes of suffering, which once known, they may help alleviate. Both use a similar *praxis*, emphasizing inwardness and self-reflection as vehicles of self-discovery. In psychoanalysis, Freud found the technique of free association to be essential to the analytic process, and described it as maintaining an even, hovering attention—a phrase that aptly describes meditation. Resistances and other defensive

"The way that mythologies work their magic is through symbols. The symbol works as an automatic button that releases energy and channels it."

—PATHWAYS TO BLISS, *page 47*

Chapter III: Society and Symbol

processes described in the analytic literature correspond nicely with the "hindrances" and "impediments" of Buddhist practice. Psychoanalysis and Buddhism are both empirical by design, and both value becoming more compassionate and empathic, acknowledging that the conditions of life are often beyond our control, but we can still be exhilarated by the experience of being alive, participating joyfully in what Campbell calls "the festival of passing forms."[1]

THE MECHANISM OF MYTHS: HOW SYMBOLS WORK

Some symbols—including the enduring, seemingly universal symbols of mythology—function as Innate Releasing Mechanisms (IRMs) or, in contemporary terms, Fixed Action Patterns (FAPs). There are many varieties of innate behaviors ranging from simple reflexes to more complex FAPs. A reflex is the simplest example of an innate behavior, and doesn't even involve the brain. One reflex you've no doubt experienced is a knee reflex, which is activated when a rubber hammer is tapped on your leg just below the kneecap, and causes your lower leg to move in a kicking-like manner. This response is made by activating circuits of neurons running between the knee and the spinal cord. The sucking reflex in infants is another example of a simple reflex.

An FAP—or, as it was known in Campbell's time, IRM—is a predictable series of actions triggered by a specific stimulus. FAPs are much more complex than simple reflexes, even though they are also autonomous and involuntary. Once an FAP is stimulated it will carry through to completion, even if the stimulus is removed. My understanding is that animals in

general (including humans and other mammals) display fixed action patterns, but rhetorical and semantic limitations in the languages of psychology and philosophy require these fields to avoid addressing human behavior in biologically instinctual ways.

Campbell, himself, doubts that IRMs (FAPs) have much influence on human behavior, and suggests that imprinting is the dominant factor in the human psyche. Imprinting is a behavior learned early in an animal's life and contributes to its survival (for example, a duckling that attaches to the first large moving object it sees and considers it to be its mother). Campbell concludes that something else, "some other constant set of experiences that almost all individuals share," gives rise to the archetypal symbols in mythologies, religions, and in the social structures of societies. That other set of experiences, he decides, are the experiences humans have during the period of infancy: the infant's relationship to its mother and father, the infant's experience of mother and father's relationship to each other, and finally, the challenges of its own psychological development and the perceptions of each developmental stage. "These universal experiences," Campbell says, "give birth to the *Elementargedanken*, the unchanging motifs of the world's cultures."[2]

SOCIETY, MYTH, AND PERSONAL DEVELOPMENT

In this section, Campbell gives us a summary of Sigmund Freud's developmental theories, in which each stage of development is associated with a particular conflict to be resolved before moving on to the next stage. Campbell covers Freud's theory of ambivalence, the Oedipal stage of development, and the genesis of dependency, an incredibly powerful experience that afflicts us at the beginning and end of our lives.

In such a brief summary it is difficult to do justice to Freudian developmental theory. Campbell is correct to describe the infant psyche as an "I want" machine[3], and as most of us can attest, longing and desire don't disappear as we age; they merely find different objects upon which to focus. The pleasure of a satisfied need is profound, but each and every need cannot possibly be satisfied, so we experience increasing amounts of tension and ambivalence between the pleasure of satisfaction and the pain of ungratified wishes.

The unfulfilled desire sinks into the unconscious and remains there as a wish, as longing. It's accompanied by a sense that what you want is prohibited to you, and this tension of wanting what you can't have generates tremendous ambivalence.

Neurosis should not be confused with psychosis, as neurosis is a more or less functional disorder while a psychosis is a complete break with reality. Campbell suggests that a neurosis may form because one is "Under the table, so to say … enjoying an experience that is forbidden by the society, and you are forbidding yourself even to know that you are enjoying it."[4] But neurosis doesn't have to result from an immoral or taboo-violating wish; neurosis may simply be the lack of an ability to adapt to one's environment or change one's life patterns in order to live more harmoniously within one's culture. Neurosis can also result from a defense against traumas such as physical or sexual abuse and the trauma of war.

Campbell also touches upon what Freud called the Oedipus

"*What distinguishes the human species from all other kinds of animals is that we are born too soon. Actually, neither the human physique nor the human psyche matures until the early twenties.*"

—PATHWAYS TO BLISS, *page 51*

Complex, which is based on Sophocles' fifth century BCE play *Oedipus Rex*. In this play, Oedipus unconsciously fulfills a prophecy by murdering his father and marrying his mother. According to Freud, the Oedipus complex arises during the phallic stage of development, around age three to six, a time when the ego is also forming, and theoretically promotes a competition between fathers and sons for the affections of the mother. Defense mechanisms provide a resolution to the Oedipal drama through repression (the blocking of ideas, desires, and impulses from the conscious mind) and identification, by which the child incorporates personality characteristics and family rules of the same-sex parent. His perceived similarity to the father relieves his irrational castration anxiety because the two of them are now in greater accord. Female children also experience what Freud called the female Oedipus attitude or the negative Oedipus complex. In women, the complex manifests in a different form, but it is similarly resolved through the daughter's identification with the mother. Freud did not call this developmental phase the Electra complex; that, in fact, was a phrase coined by C.G. Jung, with which Freud subsequently took issue, believing it to be inaccurate.

The last one and a half pages of this section address the problem of dependency, which intertwines nicely with the discussion of the Oedipus complex.

THE EGO: EAST AND WEST

Campbell begins with a brief gloss of Freud's tripartite conceptualization of consciousness, describing consciousness (that which we are aware of), the preconscious (that which we *might*

become of aware of with some directed effort), and the unconscious (material that is simply not available to us regardless of how hard we might try to recall it).

Contained in the unconscious is the id, which in Latin simply means "it," and which operates on what Freud called the pleasure principle. The id wants every wish to be satisfied immediately, with no thought to consequences. The id is largely instinctual and utilizes what Freud called primary process thinking, which is illogical, amoral, fantasy-based, and irrational. The id has no connection to objective reality.

The ego, which is only partially conscious, is conditioned by one's experience of the world. The ego's job is to navigate and negotiate reality, and it operates on the reality principle, which is an attempt to apply reason and common sense to living life. The reality principle still wants the organism to experience pleasure and has no concept of right or wrong, but its goal is to devise a realistic, world-based strategy to achieve it. Its principal concern is that of minimizing danger to the individual and creating safety. In this respect it is often in opposition to the id, which wants the pleasure of having every impulse, regardless of consequence, satisfied. But, alas, the ego is not as strong or influential as the id, and often finds itself at the mercy of the id in much the same way an inexperienced rider is at the mercy of an unruly horse.

On top of these two psychic structures is the mostly conscious superego (in German, *Uber Ich*, which literally means "over I") which is formed by internalizing cultural mores, taboos, rules, and parental influences. The superego functions as a conscience, and its primary job is to control the id's impulses, especially those impulses related to sex and aggression. The superego

Chapter III: Society and Symbol

insists on perfection and controls our sense of right and wrong. It creates feelings of guilt, failure, and shame when we fall short of our ideal self. Of course, the id, ego, and superego are theoretical concepts—metaphors pointing to deeper truths about the nature of human consciousness. They are images of psychic organs, if you will.

In this section, Campbell points out the differences in ego structure and development between the East and the West. As a reminder, in Campbell's thought the dividing line between what he calls East and West runs roughly through Persia, or modern-day Iran. East of Persia is India and the Far East, China, and Japan. West of Persia is the Near East or the Levant[5], most of Turkey, the western Mediterranean region, Europe, and the Americas.

Essentially, he sees the fundamental differences in ego development between the East and the West as the ways in which the ego forms. In the West, the ego develops a highly personal connection to the external world and gives a personal cast to the individual's experiences. One's own judgments and values are of more importance than society's. One of the great achievements of adult Western life is to become an individual with an ability to think critically about the world and make one's own judgments anchored in reason, applying wisdom distilled from personal experience.

In the East, the structure of society reflects the structure of the cosmos, the order of which provides an ideal model. As a result, the emphasis is on cancelling the ego in favor of a more impersonal, collective expression of society that mirrors the impersonality of the cosmos. Practices that teach *mokṣa*, or the renunciation of the ego, and Buddhist practices like *nekkhamma*, or

"These are the functions of the mythology, and, if they are successful, you get a sense of everything—yourself, your society, the universe, and the mystery beyond—as one great unit."

—PATHWAYS TO BLISS, *page 55*

nonattachment, are central to Eastern religious traditions and mitigate the influence of the ego. The goal is to identify oneself not with the personal and personalizing ego, but rather with the immanent yet simultaneously transcendent mystery of the Absolute, which is also the mystery of ourselves!

Points of Interest

CAMPBELL'S "HAMLET POSTURE"

In terms of what Campbell calls the "Hamlet posture,"[6] I'm not aware of Freud using that phrase in his writing, nor does he endorse the posture Campbell describes. In *The Interpretation of Dreams*, Freud, addressing variability in the nature of Oedipal issues, writes that "Shakespeare's *Hamlet* has its roots in the same soil as *Oedipus Rex*."[7] But rather than bringing the wishful fantasies to consciousness as they are in Sophocles' play, they are repressed in Shakespeare's, and Hamlet cannot take action against his father's killer (his uncle Claudius) because he identifies too much with him. In *An Outline of Psycho-Analysis*, Freud writes "Hamlet comes to grief over the task of punishing someone else for what coincided with the substance of his own Oedipus wish."[8] In other words, Hamlet's suffering was, in large part, related to the fact that someone other than himself beat him to it, if you will, and murdered his father. And even though he hates Claudius, Hamlet unconsciously identifies with him for having killed his father and married his mother.

The Oedipus complex is Freud's abstraction, just as the Hamlet posture seems to be Campbell's. As such, they are both conceptualizations, symbolic narratives of an individual's intense

striving for love. However, in strictly Freudian terms, if the desire for love is rejected or defeated, other psychic defense mechanisms may be aroused that result in the devaluing or hatred of the feminine and the feminine principle.

Campbell is not wrong to point out the problems of misogyny and sexism in patriarchal world views, but the psychodynamics are more complicated than he has represented in his very brief remarks here about the Oedipus complex. Twenty-four volumes and many thousands of pages make up *The Standard Edition of the Complete Works of Sigmund Freud*, which includes his books, other publications, and unpublished papers. Given that the Oedipus complex is elaborated in many of these individual works, and that it was a concept that Freud continually revisited until the end of his life, Campbell described it very well for such a brief summary.

Freud in Contemporary Psychoanalysis

Today, nontraditional family structures are far more widely accepted than when Freud was theorizing, and Oedipal issues no longer appear only in the ways that Freud or Campbell presented. Contemporary and post-modern psychoanalysts modify the Oedipus complex to more accurately reflect the heterogeneity of modern family life. For example, a therapist might explore the Oedipus complex from a nongendered perspective, moving away from a strictly sexual interpretation to one of socialization and learning to deal with the frustration of not getting what one wants in other areas as well. These Oedipal challenges, even in Freud's original formulation, are all related to becoming a more independent, functional member of society.

Complementary Reading from Campbell's Work

Campbell, Joseph. *Myths to Live By.* Joseph Campbell Foundation, 2011.

—. *The Inner Reaches of Outer Space: Metaphor as Myth and as Religion.* Joseph Campbell. New World Library, 2012.

Further Reading

"Fixed Action Pattern." *ScienceDirect Topics.* Accessed January 19, 2021. https://www.sciencedirect.com/topics/medicine-and-dentistry/fixed-action-pattern.

Gay, Peter. *Freud: A Life for Our Times.* J.M. Dent, 1988.

Zimmer, Heinrich Robert, and Joseph Campbell. *Myths and Symbols in Indian Art and Civilization.* Princeton University Press, 2017.

Discussion Questions

- What might be some of the differences and similarities in child and adult development between Asia, Europe, and the Americas? What might be the result of a greater understanding those differences and similarities, individually and collectively?

- In what situations do you believe Freudian theories of development are the most useful? In what situations might they be least useful?

- How have the respective geographies of Asia and Europe influenced their mythological and religious traditions?

"The guru is supposed to be an absolutely perfect pane of glass through which the light of what he has been taught shines. So this wisdom that comes through the guru comes from the ages; it has nothing to do with this moment here and now, nor with the person who is transmitting it."

—PATHWAYS TO BLISS, *page 59*

Essay Topics

- Write a paper titled "Freud and Buddhism: Common Concepts and Themes."

- Write a paper titled "The Biology of Religion."

- Write a paper titled "The Genre of Tragedy in Chinese Literature."

Creative Prompts

- What are the most important symbols in your life? Choose two or three of them, and write, paint, sculpt, or use any other art form to create a piece that includes both or all of them.

- Rewrite Hamlet's "To be, or not to be" soliloquy imagining that Hamlet is well-versed in Sophocles' play *Oedipus Rex* and/or Freud's idea of the Oedipus complex.

- Find a movie from a culture different from your own. Watch the movie, then create a piece of art in response to it.

NOTES

1 Joseph Campbell, *The Masks of God: Primitive Mythology*, Secker & Warburg, 1960, 25.
2 Joseph Campbell, *Pathways to Bliss*, 48–49.
3 Ibid, 49.

4 Ibid, 50.

5 In contemporary use, the term *Levant* is used mostly in the fields of archaeology and history. The use of the term is attractive to scholars (and others) who wish to avoid the biblical and nationalist implications of other geographic descriptors such as Syria-Palestine, and more geographically inclusive of areas that typically lie outside the Middle East, such as Turkey and Cyprus.

6 Campbell, *Pathways to Bliss,* 50.

7 Ivan Smith, *Freud—Complete Works,* 2010, 743.

8 Ibid, p. 4999.

Chapter IV
Myth and the Self

Chapter Summary

In this chapter Campbell discusses C.G. Jung's theories of Analytical Psychology. In the first section of this chapter, "Jung and the Polarities of Personality," Campbell briefly describes how Jung differs from Freud in his theoretical conceptualization of psyche, then introduces some major features of Jung's theory regarding the structures of the unconscious such as introversion and extroversion, and the four basic functions of thinking, feeling, intuition, and sensation. Although Campbell found Jung's approach better suited to the study of mythology, he never seemed to lose an appreciation for Freud and the insights of psychoanalysis.

The remainder of the chapter focuses on Jung's concept of archetypes. Campbell touches on a bit of biographical detail and then discusses some important Jungian archetypes, including the self, the shadow, and the anima and animus, as well as the concept of personae. Campbell does a good job of explaining these concepts, and I will offer some elaborations and clarifications as well.

JUNG AND THE POLARITIES OF PERSONALITY

In this section, Campbell discusses what Jung termed the "general basic attitudes" of the psyche. ("The Type Problem in Human Character" (Volume 6 of *The Collected Works of C.G. Jung*). Perhaps as a way to bridge the gap from another former

Freudian, Alfred Adler (whose theory emphasized feelings of inferiority and the striving for power) to Jung, Campbell uses distinctly Freudian terms of sex and power to describe the basic psychological attitudes that Jung called introversion and extroversion.[1] The extrovert is oriented outward and feels more comfortable and energized in the world of objects and other people, while the introvert is more comfortable and energized by solitude and reflection. Campbell rightly points out that "every individual is both, with an accent on one or the other."[2] In fact, extroversion and introversion are in a compensatory relationship to each other; if one's consciousness is introverted, one's unconscious will be extroverted, and vice-versa. When the unconscious attitude breaks through, one is for a time unrecognizable as the person others would say they know, which can cause serious difficulties in relationships between spouses, parents and children, friends, and even with sociocultural norms and expectations.

On a related point, when we find ourselves out of balance, psychically speaking, the inferior personality emerges and "You are out of control; the inferior character has taken over. It is more primitive than the developed side of the personality."[3] In fact, Jung writes that the lowest levels of the inferior personality "are indistinguishable from the instinctuality of an animal."[4] Campbell notes that Jung called such a reversal of personality an *enantiodromia* which, Jung explains, means the tendency of things to turn into their opposites and to run counter to what was previously the norm. Jung borrowed this word from Heraclitus, who used it "to designate the play of opposites in the course of events—the view that everything that exists turns into its opposite."[5]

Campbell gives a nice summary of Jung's four functions that operate on the basic psychological attitudes of introversion and

"*Ethics and social mores are internalized as part of the persona order, and Jung tells us that you must take that lightly, too. Just remember, Adam and Eve fell when they learned the difference between good and evil. So the way to get back is not to know the difference.*"

—PATHWAYS TO BLISS, *page 72*

extroversion. A psychological function is a form of psychological activity that maintains the same qualities even though conditions, both mental and physical, may change. A function is a manifestation of the life force, which similarly remains constant in nature. Jung notes that the thinking and feeling functions are rational, while sensation and intuition are irrational functions.

THE ARCHETYPES OF THE COLLECTIVE UNCONSCIOUS

In his familiar, accessible way, Campbell describes archetypes as "certain fixed structures" in the human mind. And these structures "evolved as a part of the human mind, just as the hand or eye evolved. Like the hand and eye, almost all of us share these structures in common. [Jung] therefore called them the archetypes of the collective unconscious."[6] Jung took the word *archetype* from its Greek usage, which means "original pattern," and meant it to characterize certain instinctive images and patterns in the deep, collective unconscious. Archetypes are not "inherited" ideas, but are rather inherited potentialities or modes of psychic functioning.[7] Jung also referred to the archetypes as psychic organs.

The archetypes have a dark side as well as a light side and emerge on many psychic levels and in a variety of forms. They tend to accommodate various psychological situations, and yet they remain the same in their basic structure and meaning—much in the same way a line of music may be transposed into another key. In the unconscious, which uses a picture language (such as in dreams, fantasies, visions, etc.) the archetypes appear in personified or symbolic images. Jung believed we cannot say with any authority what these archetypes mean, and thought that the best we can do with them is translate them into another metaphorical statement, a different way to make use of them in a more personally meaningful way. For instance, a dream in which a dog is trying to bite you might mean different things to you and, say, your friend. You might associate the dream image to your intuition, or something you're currently unconscious of which is trying to motivate you. Your friend might associate the same image to their overly critical, often hostile, mother.

Campbell speaks to many of the most significant and familiar archetypes, such as the self, the shadow, and the anima and animus. He also discusses Jung's notion of the persona, taken from the Latin word for mask. Personas are masks we create in our efforts to adapt to the external circumstances of our lives, or for our own personal convenience. A persona is by no means similar to individuality or some sort of genuine or authentic self. It is very important for a person to be able to distinguish between when and where donning the mask is appropriate and when it is not. To some degree, the persona is a conscious choice, and wearing it often creates tension with the deep, unconscious self. As Campbell notes, when one is playing a part, a role, one shouldn't "take it too damned seriously. The persona is merely the mask you're wearing for this game."[8]

Campbell also spends some time discussing the shadow. He refers to the shadow as a "blind spot in your nature … It is made up of the desires and ideas within you that you are repressing."[9] Jung says the shadow is "an inferior component of the personality and is consequently repressed through intensive resistance."[10] There exists, however, a persistent tension between consciousness and the unconscious shadow contents. In the same paragraph, Jung poetically describes the conscious mind as being on top with the

"Now, typically, all these archetypes come out personified in myths and dreams. We personify the mystery of the universe as God."

—PATHWAYS TO BLISS, *page 74*

shadow underneath, "and just as high always longs for low and hot for cold, so all consciousness ... seeks its unconscious opposite, lacking which it is doomed to stagnation, congestion, and ossification. Life is born only of the spark of opposites."

Campbell also addresses the anima and animus archetypes. The anima and animus are archetypal personifications of the soul and are both experienced by all of us. In C.G. Jung's view, a man's anima takes on a generally a feminine form, while a woman's animus is some sort of masculine form. This has, over the years, become one of Jung's more problematic theories because it assumes such a reductive view of gender. This gendering is underscored by Jung's assertion of the primacy of opposites. If a man functions in the world in a very masculine way, he must have a very feminine inner world. This *oppositorum* holds true, Jung says, for women as well; if they present a very feminine persona, they will have a very masculine animus.[11]

Campbell makes a comment in his discussion of the anima archetype that has, perhaps, more resonance for a contemporary audience than it had for the audience he was addressing: "The interesting thing is that—biologically and psychologically—we have both sexes in us; yet in all human societies, one is allowed to accent only one. The other is internalized within us."[12] The societal expectation that one may only accent one or the other gender, and furthermore, that the gender one accents is the gender one must forever-after embrace, causes a great deal of controversy and suffering in contemporary culture.

Because the anima/animus archetype functions unconsciously, it is easily projected onto real, flesh-and-blood men and women, and we fall in love believing the object of our affection embodies our

"The world is a constellation of imperfections, and you, perhaps, are the most imperfect of all. By your love for the world you name it accurately and without pity and love what you have thus named."

—PATHWAYS TO BLISS, *page 78*

own inner ideal. The fact that projection determines our romantic relationships is probably unavoidable, and the way Campbell treats that in this section is quite lovely. He proposes that when we inevitably discover our partner fails to live up to our own projected ideal the answer is, rather than recrimination and accusation, compassion. Through compassion we can withdraw all our unconscious projections; through compassion, we recognize that we're only human, and humans are imperfect creatures. With compassion we can learn to have, as Cary Grant says to Kathryn Hepburn in *The Philadelphia Story*, "some small regard for human frailty,"[13] a human frailty that cries out to be loved.

Campbell finishes this chapter by looking at four crises that, as he puts it, "can bring about a very serious enantiodromia."[14] The first potential crisis is the movement from one developmental stage of life to another without recognizing the fact that one is no longer the same, that the conditions of one's life are no longer the same, and the crisis arises from one either neglecting that fact, or refusing to recognize it.

The second potential crisis Campbell identifies is in some respects a developmental crisis as well, but of a specific kind. A crisis precipitating an enantiodromia may be caused by continuing to drive and push and expend libido in the same way one has always done, failing to recognize that it may be the time of one's life to relax, to give up the idea that one can be master of the universe and instead just enjoy the fruits of one's efforts.

The third type of crisis Campbell describes is a "loss of confidence in your moral ideals."[15] This often may take the form of a spiritual crisis in which what one has always believed to be true is revealed to be inadequate at best, and at worst, a lie. The ideals one had once believed to be one's moral and spiritual foundation no longer explain, no longer console, no longer reassure. Things fall apart, Yeats tells us, and the center cannot hold.[16] The band R.E.M. captured the essence of this crisis in their song "Losing My Religion."[17]

The fourth crisis—and, from Campbell's perspective, the most serious—is the challenge to one's moral reasoning of being forced to make an "intolerable decision"[18] between two equally horrible options. This can be very difficult for the ego to accept. Campbell admonishes us "*not* to identify these morals with cosmic truths,"[19] meaning societal morals to which the persona conforms. Laws, moral injunctions, and standards are to be examined in individual circumstances and not applied in a blanket, thoughtless manner. The individual must learn to live by their own lights, their own judgements, their own passions. This is what Campbell meant by following your bliss; it's not an easy, comfortable path, and it often feels as though one is swimming against the tide. "In effect," Campbell says, "the individual must learn to live by his or her own myth."[20]

Points of Interest

FREUD AND JUNG

Sigmund Freud, born in 1856, was nearly a generation older than C.G. Jung, born in 1875, and was an important figure in Jung's life. Freud and Jung were both physicians, but with very different interests and focuses. Freud was, first and foremost, biologically oriented. His work on brains and nervous systems of various species laid an important foundation for the discovery of the neuron.

Just how important the biological perspective was to Freud is demonstrated by his gloss of Napoleon, which occurs at least twice in his collected writings, saying that biology is destiny.

C.G. Jung, while well-schooled in the principles of biology, was far more interested in the phenomenon of psychological experience. Jung's dissertation, published in 1903, was titled *On the Psychology and Pathology of So-Called Occult Phenomena*. It was an analysis of the "mediumship" of Jung's younger cousin Hélène Preiswerk. No doubt his mother's often strange, disturbing behaviors and uncanny utterances stimulated Jung's lifelong interest in the various manifestations and expressions of the human psyche.

Freud and Jung were aware of one another's work, and initially through correspondence, began to develop a professional and personal alliance. They worked closely, and generally within Freud's system of psychoanalysis, for six years or so, and had an intense personal relationship until Jung published his increasingly divergent theories regarding libido in *The Psychology of the Unconscious* in 1912. Their increasing theoretical and personal conflict finally led to a complete break in 1913.

THE COLLECTIVE UNCONSCIOUS

The idea of the Collective Unconscious is a significant innovation by Jung, and sets him apart from Freud, who thought that the unconscious was comprised of mostly personal, repressed contents. The Collective Unconscious is a warehouse of primordial images and psychic forms inherited from previous generations of human beings. You can think of it as holding images and tropes passed down to us from our ancestors. The Collective Unconscious is the inheritance of every human being regardless of ethnicity or geographic region.

THE BOON OF THE SHADOW

The shadow is often one of the first archetypes to emerge in therapy as people begin to question why they are uncomfortable with their own inner world, why some people dislike them, why they have so much anxiety, why they simultaneously hate and need rules to live by, and so forth. When therapeutic work begins to integrate the shadow, and patients realize there is a significant aspect of themselves of which they are unaware, which feels alien to themselves yet is tremendously influential in their lives, they are, at first, shocked. But soon they recognize that the discovery of their shadow hides a boon, because the shadow contains more than just threatening impulses or desires. The darkness of the shadow also contains strengths, abilities, knowledge, and emotions one didn't realize one possessed. Understood this way, shadow work is vital to a greater sense of wholeness, and moves one along the path of individuation, contributing to psychological integration, or the harmonious coming together of the whole psyche.

DEGENDERING THE ANIMA

The anima is an incredibly complex archetype, both in terms of its bewildering, enigmatic nature, as well as its tendency to form complexes around itself. Anima is more complicated than simply the feminine ideal in the masculine unconscious; in fact, one may imagine the anima as a personification of the soul for everyone, regardless of gender. Therefore, it is one's most inner personality, related to inner psychic processes of which we are largely unconscious. In this view, the anima exists in opposition to one's outer attitude or outer personality, which is the persona, and contains all those qualities or elements that the outer personality lacks.

The mother is the first anima encounter we have, and personifies the entire unconscious. In *Faust*, for example, Goethe refers to the realm of the mothers from which Faust returns with the ideal form of beauty, Helen of Troy. Of course, forgetting that she is an ideal form and not a flesh and blood woman, Faust falls in love with her as though she might be any other woman. As is typical of anima projections, they cannot be the foundation of a relationship because the idealized projection simply can't be maintained over time. As if to illustrate that fact, Goethe shows the sorrowful Helen eventually disappearing in a mist, returning to Hades.

INTOLERABLE DECISIONS AND MORAL DEVELOPMENT

As the psychologist Lawrence Kohlberg demonstrated in his theory of moral development[21], one is not always "free" to make the appropriate moral decision at the appropriate time. For Kohlberg, moral development consisted of three levels, each level building upon the previous one and split into two stages.

Kohlberg called the first stage preconventional morality. This stage consists of basic understandings of right and wrong. A person is good if they are not punished, and if they are punished, they believe they must have done something wrong.

Preconventional morality may sometimes advance to the point that one recognizes that different people may have different codes of conduct.

The next level is conventional morality, which is characterized by acceptance of social rules about what is right and wrong. Initially in this stage, the individual tries to be good to gain the approval of others. Later, the individual places the great value on following rules and not breaking the law.

In postconventional morality, Kohlberg's third and final stage, one understands and incorporates humanistic ethical principles. Initially, one realizes that even when laws exist to facilitate the greatest good for the greatest number of people, these laws may also work against the interests of some individuals. Later the individual embraces universal human rights, equality in justice, and their own moral guidelines that may or may not be embraced by others. They are willing to diverge from conventional morality even if it means social disapproval or imprisonment. Few people reach this stage of moral development, but it is what Campbell urges us to aim for.

Complementary Reading from Campbell's Work

Campbell, Joseph. *The Flight of the Wild Gander: Explorations in the Mythical Dimension.* New World Library, 2002.

Further Reading

Bair, Deirdre. *Jung: A Biography*. Little, Brown, 2004.

Jung, C.G. *Archetypes of the Collective Unconscious*. Princeton University Press, 1969.

Nietzsche, Friedrich. *Daybreak: Thoughts on the Prejudices of Morality*. Cambridge University Press, 1997.

McGuire, William, editor. *The Freud/Jung Letters: The Correspondence between Sigmund Freud and C.G. Jung*. Princeton University Press, 1974.

Discussion Questions

- What does Joseph Campbell mean when he says that the individual must learn to live by their own myth? Do you know any people who have done this? Do you know any people who haven't?

- There are many ways to become more conscious of one's own shadow, but these techniques require unflinching honesty with oneself. How are you selfish, for instance? What are the qualities you hate in other people? The things we hate about others are often things we hate about ourselves. How do I justify my actions, and what do I do when I can't? These are only a few ways to meet one's shadow. What others can you think of?

- How did Freud and Jung differ in defining the concept of libido? Which definition appeals to you more, and why?

Essay Topics

- Using two to three movies as examples, explore the differences between a postconventional morality and amoral or antisocial behaviors.

- Using one of your all-time favorite movies, describe the use of archetypes in the film.

- What is the nature of, and the use of, persona in the social media presence of online influencers? How might this affect the influencers themselves, and those who follow them? The influenced, so to speak.

Creative Prompts

- Choose a fictional character you feel you understand well. Write a story in which their shadow takes over their persona.

- Imagine that your persona and your anima could communicate via text messages. Write the conversation between these two voices as they try to decide what to have for supper.

- Using a medium you don't normally work in, create an expression of an intolerable decision between two equally impossible choices. Extend the work past the immediate decision to explore the results of whatever happens.

Chapter IV: Myth and the Self

NOTES

1 For a deeper understanding of introversion, extroversion, and psychological types, see Jung's work *Psychological Types*, which is Volume Six of the *Collected Works of C.G. Jung*.
2 Joseph Campbell, *Pathways to Bliss*, 64.
3 Ibid, 64.
4 C.G. Jung, *Aion*, §370.
5 Jung, *Psychological Types*, §709.
6 Campbell, *Pathways to Bliss*, 68.
7 For a clear explanation of the important elements of Jungian analytical psychology, see *The Psychology of C.G. Jung*, by Jolande Jacobi (Yale University Press, 1973).
8 Campbell, *Pathways to Bliss*, 72.
9 Ibid, 73.
10 Jung, *On the Psychology of the Unconscious*, §78.
11 Accepting this structure, then, one cannot avoid the thought that one's anima must have an animus, and that animus must have an anima, and so on. It's a tale of infinite regression similar to the familiar notion of turtles all the way down. In the beginning of his book *A Brief History of Time*, Stephen Hawking tells the following story: "A well-known scientist (some say it was Bertrand Russell) once gave a public lecture on astronomy. He described how the earth orbits around the sun and how the sun, in turn, orbits around the centre of a vast collection of stars called our galaxy. At the end of the lecture, a little old lady at the back of the room got up and said: 'What you have told us is rubbish. The world is really a flat plate supported on the back of a giant tortoise.' The scientist gave a superior smile before replying, 'What is the tortoise standing on?' 'You're very clever, young man, very clever,' said the old lady. 'But it's turtles all the way down.'"

12 Campbell, *Pathways to Bliss*, 75.
13 George Cukor, *The Philadelphia Story*, MGM, 1940.
14 Campbell, *Pathways to Bliss*, 80.
15 Ibid, 81.
16 W.B. Yeats, "The Second Coming," *The Dial*, 1921.
17 R.E.M., "Losing My Religion," *Out of Time*, 1991.
18 Campbell, *Pathways to Bliss*, 82.
19 Ibid, 83.
20 Ibid, 83.
21 With his doctoral dissertation, numerous scholarly articles, and books such as *The Psychology of Moral Development, The Philosophy of Moral Development*, and *Moral Stages: A Current Formulation and a Response to Critics (Contributions to Human Development, Vol. 10)*, Dr. Kohlberg has advanced and fleshed out Piaget's theory of moral development to a remarkable degree.

Chapter V
Personal Myth

Chapter Summary

This chapter is important to the essence of this book as it gives us one of the most viable, adaptive, and therapeutic ways to understand myth. Personal myth is a concept that is defined in various ways by various people, but personal engagement with myth as described by Joseph Campbell is a marvelously creative, practical, and beneficial way of working with myth. Our introduction to Jung in the previous chapter will be an invaluable aid to understanding what Campbell considered to be personal mythology.

JUNG: WHAT MYTH DO I LIVE BY?

This section explores personal mythology framed by the question Jung asked himself. This was an especially important question for Jung to have posed because, as Campbell notes, "Mythological images are the images by which the consciousness is put in touch with the unconscious." Furthermore, when you ignore them, "you are out of touch with your own deepest part."[1] The more out of touch we are with our own "deepest part," the more elusive is the sense of meaning in one's life, without which life feels somehow impoverished. To the extent that we can use myth to become more conscious, we can access a deeper, more vibrant experience of life, so life appears less alien and strange, more comfortable, more understandable. We are more aware of what Jung called our "indispensable place in the great process of being."[2]

Chapter V: Personal Myth

Early in this section, Campbell makes a statement that may be surprising: "It's my belief that there is no longer a single mythology operating for everybody in any one country, let alone across Western civilization … social order today is essentially secular in character … We don't explain our laws in mythological terms."[3] There is no longer a common mythology that shapes, defines, and determines our lives. We humans are too diverse, too populous, too interconnected, and too well informed about the world for monolithic mythologies to explain our existence and the universe. What's more, Campbell thought that there will not "be anything like a unified mythology for mankind for a long time, if there ever is again."[4]

Campbell then poses a challenging question: What, he asks, would inspire one to go on living if everything that was most important, most dear, most meaningful, were taken away? What would keep one from losing one's mind, dropping out of life, or even ending it? What would allow one to continue to go on? "What is the great thing for which you would sacrifice your life? What makes you do what you do; what is the call of your life to you—do you know it?"[5] The old mythic traditions used to provide answers to these types of questions. Now we are left to our own devices to answer them, and each individual must find their own answer.

These are the kinds of questions that make us uncomfortable, that might keep us awake at three o'clock in the morning, because there are no easy, completely satisfying answers. Often we answer these questions by not thinking about them, and instead we create lives of security, status, or success in work and relationships, but these things are, Campbell insists, "exactly the values that a mythically inspired person *doesn't* live for."[6] A person who lives in the grip of passion, who has a calling—who is, one might say, following bliss—cares not at all for those concerns.

People who are seized by an idea or a vision live in such a way that everything pales in significance to the guiding principle that dominates their thoughts and organizes their life. However, it's important to acknowledge that one who lives this way (Campbell cites the example of Gauguin)—the geniuses, the culture heroes among us—are frequently problematic in relationship to others. As Friedrich Nietzsche noted throughout *Human, All Too Human: A Book for Free Spirits*, people can be "bound" by their commitments to family, to decency, tradition, and even bound by a love of the place in which they grew up.[7] These connections are nothing to scoff at, and may bring a sense of meaning and value to one's life, but sometimes one's passion—one's bliss—overcomes one.

The qualities of individuals who follow their bliss, as Campbell puts it, are the same qualities of those whom Nietzsche calls "free spirits." Many of us needn't "live dangerously," as Nietzsche elsewhere exhorts us,[8] but we might benefit from letting go of neurotic concerns about security, money, prestige, and one's own lovability. We can find the courage to take more risks, especially in the areas of our passions, than we may normally be inclined to do. Even if we don't want to abandon our family, or country, or every comfort, it is nonetheless a useful metaphorical ideal. Rather than take Nietzsche literally, we can be inspired to lower our defenses, be more comfortable with the discomfort of the unknown, and step outside a narrowly defined life. He is urging us to live thoughtfully, reflectively, and with feeling.

"Mythological images are the images by which the consciousness is put in touch with the unconscious. That's what they are. When you don't have your mythological images, or when your consciousness rejects them for some reason or other, you are out of touch with your own deepest part."

—PATHWAYS TO BLISS, *page 87*

Entertaining the metaphorical idea to live dangerously (entertaining "dangerous" ideas is, in fact, a way of living more dangerously) opens the door to a mythic world, an enchanted world, one that pulls us out of our prosaic, domestic existences and familiar "rational" thoughts. This is a powerfully creative psychological perspective that Campbell insists is responsible for great cultural innovations, perhaps even civilization itself! For "That awakening of awe, that awakening of zeal, is the beginning [and] that's what pulls people together."[9]

Campbell again references Maslow's *Hierarchy of Needs*,[10] and he writes, "Two things pull people together: aspiration and terror."[11] Instinctively we know this to be true; in the United States, our entire political system is predicated upon this reality.

THE FOUR FUNCTIONS OF MYTHOLOGY IN TRADITION AND TODAY

In the previous section I mentioned Campbell's understanding that we no longer have the support of a living, functioning mythology. Of his four functions of myth, only the first function—awakening a sense of awe, mystery, and gratitude—and the fourth function—the pedagogical, psychological function—are still influential in contemporary "myth." The other two functions of myth have been taken over by science and secular social institutions. The fourth function of myth, the psychological function, is the focus of this section. Mythology provides very effective psychology because, as Campbell writes, there is a "wonderful accord between the exterior and interior worlds, and it's not as though God had breathed anything into us; the gods we know are projections of our own fantasies, our own consciousnesses, our own deep being."[12]

Myth facilitates what Jung called "the co-operation between conscious and unconscious." The symbols of myth are grounded in the archetypes of the unconscious, but their forms and specific content are filled out by the individual's conscious experiences and ideas. It would be a mistake to understand oneself in terms of one myth or another; it is more psychologically useful to think about oneself mythically—imaginatively, metaphorically, and symbolically. While it's certainly tempting to identify with one figure or another from myth, that is largely an attraction of the ego and conscious preference.

Instead, thinking mythically about oneself requires one to patiently and carefully notice the patterns of living that repeat in one's life, the way one thinks and responds in various situations, watching with fascination that which emerges from the depths of oneself. Thinking mythically means to be alert to the possibility of recognizing the deeply unconscious mythic images, symbols, and narratives that the psyche is putting forth. This is best accomplished without any preconceptions or fears about what might emerge. Jung explains:

> The psyche is not of today; its ancestry goes back many millions of years. Individual consciousness is only the flower and the fruit of a season, sprung from the perennial rhizome beneath the earth; and it would find itself in better accord with the truth if it took the existence of the rhizome into its calculations. For the root matter is the mother of all things.[13]

There is a great deal of difference between recognizing that myth can be personally beneficial, and personalizing myth. Personalizing the archetypal images of myth is similar to a butterfly collector pinning a butterfly in a shadow box: The object of beauty, fascination, and awe is no longer alive. Likewise, the myth is reduced to a psychic tchotchke, an object of bemusement, in which a startlingly alive beauty no longer resides. As with the pinned, dead butterfly, we can no longer follow the myth on its unhurried, organic, meandering way, leading us away from the comfortable environs of domesticity and deeper into, not just the natural world, but our own fathomless nature and the sublime discoveries it holds. (I should point out that the Greek homonym, *psyche,* is used to denote both butterfly and soul.)

Thinking mythically, thinking not of archetypes but rather of the archetypal, one finds the real power of myth. One wakes up, as it were, and finds oneself less constrained, less burdened, and less in opposition to the complexities and limitations of life. Mythic thinking opens the doors of perception to astonishment, to contentment, to life with its full range of emotion and experience. Your personal myth is no longer a myth—a collection of sacred, guiding stories; it has become your life, and you are "transparent to the transcendent."[14] I must ironically admit to struggling with that phrase, "transparent to the transcendent," until I remembered Ralph Waldo Emerson's essay, *Nature,* in which he writes of becoming "a transparent eyeball":

> In the woods, we return to reason and faith. There I feel that nothing can befall me in life—no disgrace, no calamity (leaving me my eyes), which nature cannot repair. Standing on the bare ground—my head bathed by the blithe air and uplifted into infinite space—all mean egotism vanishes. I become a transparent eyeball; I am nothing; I see all; the currents of the Universal Being circulate through me; I am part or parcel of God.[15]

"Well, as I've said, mythologies are basically the same everywhere. Consequently, mythic images do not refer primarily to historical events. They come from the psyche and talk to the psyche; their primary reference is to the psyche—to the spirit, as we call it—and not to a historical event."

—PATHWAYS TO BLISS, *page 92*

Chapter V: Personal Myth

This is, I have no doubt, exactly what Joseph Campbell meant by becoming transparent to the transcendent. "In this way," Campbell writes, "you will find, live, and become a realization of your own personal myth."[16]

Points of Interest

CONTEMPORARY MYTHS?

Sometimes I hear people, even mythologists, talk of contemporary myths or contemporary mythologies. Even among those who value Joseph Campbell's work, people say that modern mythmakers are poets, artists[17], storytellers of all varieties. Garrisons of New Age "gurus" emphasize mythic imagery and narratives. People speak of the movie *Star Wars* as a contemporary myth, and some *Star Trek* fans import the ethos of Starfleet into their personal lives. But in my view, these are not new mythologies. They are merely examples of what Sheldon Wolin called "post-mythic structures," which emit the hint of archaic bewilderment and fascination, awe, and religious observance "in the midst of a modernizing society which, by its own self-understanding, is committed to the systematic extirpation of mythical thought."[18]

Countless other examples of post-mythic structures operate in contemporary life, ranging from evangelical fundamentalism to the uniquely American notions of rugged individualism, and the vague insistence that the United States be imagined as the "shining city on the hill." These contemporary narratives and images are not the spontaneous, archetypal, unconscious expressions of myth, but are instead remnants of ancient mythologies inserted into contemporary life and society.

Chapter V: Personal Myth

Contemporary life is largely dominated by STEM—science, technology, engineering, and math—disciplines that are indifferent to mythic thought. But relying solely upon reason and intellect is as problematic as undisciplined, unreflected belief and idiosyncratic beliefs. Jung thought that

> The more the critical reason dominates, the more impoverished life becomes; but the more of the unconscious, and the more of myth we are capable of making conscious, the more of life we integrate. Overvalued reason has this in common with political absolutism: under its dominion the individual is pauperized.[19]

Terror and the Sublime

It may be helpful to think about what Campbell calls "terror" as the sublime. There are three thinkers, Pseudo-Longinus, Edmund Burke, and Immanuel Kant who, taken together, have largely articulated the depth and breadth of the sublime. Burke convincingly insists that terror opens one to the sublime, but he doesn't really demonstrate why the experience of terror is sublime and, like Longinus, he relegates the sublime to the external, natural world. Kant describes the experience of the sublime as more of an inner experience, much closer to what Campbell calls bliss: "Thus, instead of the object, it is rather the cast of mind appreciating it that we have to estimate as sublime."[20]

For Kant, the sublime has two main dimensions: first, one of power, and second, one of magnitude. Sublime encounters are overwhelmingly powerful, and facing them we are compelled to feel our existential fragility and terror. Additionally, the sublime

113

is of a magnitude so vast that we simply cannot wrap our minds around it. But yet, at some point in the confrontation with the sublime we recognize that we are a part of *it* and this "mental movement," to use Kant's phrase, a kind of mutual interpenetration of the self and the sublime, begins to lend comprehension to the incomprehensible. It is as if, in an attempt to understand it, we reach into the sublime and it likewise reaches into us. Through this mental movement a kind of knowledge or understanding is generated and one begins to identify with and partake of the power of the sublime object, thereby transcending our terror and recognizing that we are ourselves the origin of the power we face.

Regarding the function of the sublime, the poet Percy Bysshe Shelley remarked that it persuades us to forsake the easy for the harder pleasures. The sublime is precisely, I think, that seizure that Campbell mentions frequently in this section when he discusses "that something that pulls you out of yourself, beyond yourself, and beyond all rational patterns."[21]

In other words, returning once more to Campbell, "you find in yourself that which moves you."[22] In doing so, it is important to be honest about what stage of life you're in so that one is not beholden to a nonexistent fantasy image of oneself on one hand, nor a nostalgic longing for the person one used to be on the other. One also runs into trouble when we try to hold on to a persona that no longer relates to the circumstances or flow of one's present life. One can't remain young forever and we must eventually surrender to the passage of time. Nevertheless, if we can acknowledge aging and eventual death with equanimity and good humor, we preserve a spark of eternal youth.

"There's nothing you can do that's more important than being fulfilled. You become a sign, you become a signal, transparent to transcendence; in this way, you will find, live, and become a realization of your own personal myth."

—PATHWAYS TO BLISS, *page 108*

Complementary Reading from Campbell's Work

Campbell, Joseph. *A Joseph Campbell Companion: Reflections on the Art of Living*. Joseph Campbell Foundation, 2011.

—. *The Hero with a Thousand Faces*. New World Library, 2008.

Further Reading

Jung, C.G. *Memories, Dreams, Reflections*. Knopf Doubleday, 2011.

—. *Symbols of Transformation*. Trans. R.F.C. Hull. Routledge, 2014.

Von Franz, Marie-Louise. *Shadow and Evil in Fairy Tales*. Shambhala, 1995.

Discussion Questions

- Why do you think that Joseph Campbell says there won't be anything like a unified mythology for mankind for a long time, if there ever is again? In what ways do you agree and disagree with his view?

- What is the role of history in mythology? Provide two or three examples.

- How many personae can a single individual have? How might personae help and hinder someone in their life?

Essay topics

- Explore the scientific function of myth in antiquity. How did the scientific function of myth influence different societies? Write deeply about one example, or compare and contrast three different societies.

- How could mythology be helpful in working through the crises one may face in life, especially at the transitional points from one stage of development to the next? How could mythology be harmful?

- Explore the possibility that archetypes are neurological structures.

Creative Prompts

- Think back to an experience in your life. Rewrite that event except with characters from myth playing the roles. Feel free to reimagine the event as you write.

- Think of an event from myth. Rewrite that event except with realistic, present-day mortals as characters.

- Write, paint, sculpt, dance, or sing about an experience that filled you with awe.

NOTES

1 Joseph Campbell, *Pathways to Bliss*, 87.
2 C.G. Jung, *Memories, Dreams, Reflections* (Knopf Doubleday, 2011), 310.
3 Joseph Campbell, *Pathways to Bliss*, 86.
4 Ibid, 87.
5 Ibid, 88.
6 Ibid, 89.
7 Friedrich Nietzsche, *Human, All Too Human: A Book for Free Spirits* (Cambridge University Press, 1986).
8 —, *The Gay Science* (Random House, 1974), 161.
9 Joseph Campbell, *Pathways to Bliss*, 91.
10 Maslow used the terms *physiological, safety, belonging and love, social needs* or *esteem*, and *self-actualization* to describe the patterns that generally inspire human motivations.
11 Joseph Campbell, *Pathways to Bliss*, 91.
12 Ibid, 106.
13 C.G. Jung, *Symbols of Transformation*, trans. R.F.C. Hull (Routledge, 2014), xxiv.
14 Joseph Campbell, *Pathways to Bliss*, 108.
15 Ralph Waldo Emerson, *The Complete Essays and Other Writings of Ralph Waldo Emerson* (Random House, 1940), 6.
16 Joseph Campbell, *Pathways to Bliss*, 108.
17 I take pains here to point out that Joseph Campbell did not explicitly say that artists are the mythmakers of modern, contemporary life, even though many people infer just that from his remarks to Bill Moyers in the *Joseph Campbell and the Power of Myth* interviews. Not every artist is making myth, and not every artistic production is mythic. But the misperception that all artists are making myth persists like smoke over the water and adds to the perception that myth is a more or less quotidian

phenomenon. The actual exchange was this, in Program Three, "The First Storytellers" (1988):

> *Moyers:* You mean, our artists are the mythmakers of our day?
> *Campbell:* The mythmakers in earlier days were the counterparts of our artists.
> *Moyers:* They drew the paintings on the wall—
> *Campbell:* Yes.
> *Moyers:* —they performed the rituals.
> *Campbell:* There's an old romantic idea, in German, *das Volktische*. That's that the poetry of the traditional cultures and the ideas come out of the folk. They do not; they come out of an elite experience, the experience of people, particularly gifted, whose ears are open to the song of the universe. And they speak to the folk and there is an answer from the folk which is then received, there's an interaction, but the first impulse comes from above, not from below, in the shaping of folk traditions.

18 Sheldon Wolin, "Postmodern Politics and the Absence of Myth," *Social Research* 52, no. 2 (1985), 217–39.
19 C.G. Jung, *Memories, Dreams, Reflections*, 363.
20 Immanuel Kant, *The Critique of Judgment* (Clarendon Press, 1952), 104.
21 Joseph Campbell, *Pathways to Bliss*, 91.
22 Ibid, 99.

Chapter VI
The Self as Hero

Chapter Summary

The entire thrust of this chapter is to find within yourself a hero. Campbell begins by exploring how to discover your own destiny. Beginning in this way, Campbell seems to be suggesting that discovering your destiny is, in fact, the heroic act. He equates your destiny with your myth, particularly if we understand myth as a way of thinking that encourages cooperation between conscious and unconscious processes.

Campbell suggests two ways to discover one's destiny. First, he says, we can realize our destiny in retrospect, remembering the events of our lives. He refers to the early nineteenth century German philosopher Arthur Schopenhauer, who reflects that our lives can seem to have had a plot when we look back over them.

Campbell says you can also figure out your destiny, your myth, while you are living it. Jung's methods—dream work, observing and inquiring into one's conscious choices, journaling, and paying attention to the stories that resonate and reappear—are very helpful in this task. These activities create greater balance between the conscious and unconscious, and a deeper, stronger sense of self. These are also ways to discover elements of the hero's adventure, or what James Joyce called the monomyth, in your own life. Campbell's explanation of the hero's journey[1] is what he calls "an archetypal story that springs from the collective unconscious. Its motifs can appear not only in myth and literature, but, if you are sensitive to it, in the working out of the plot of your own life."[2]

All the different stages of the hero's journey you may have read about in books by screenwriters or artists can be distilled down to three: Separation, Initiation, and Return. That's all there is to it. Each stage has its variations and its related myths, but the hero's adventure is not a program, it's a psychological process. Because it's a process, we go through it more than once—many times more, usually. The hero's journey describes how we grow, and accordingly, we will find ourselves living in this archetypal pattern each time we enter a new stage of life: marriage or divorce, new job, moving to a new city, and so on. Anytime we are forced outside our comfort zones we will find ourselves in the hero's adventure.

"The first stage is leaving where you are."[3] Separation. Departure. I think of this as leave-taking, and I believe it is a primary archetypal feature of human experience. All things flow, said Heraclitus, nothing remains the same or holds its form forever. Change, the leavings and the losses, the growings and the groanings, the knowings and the no-ings, altered states of consciousness, deaths, births, new challenges, are all the fabric of our brief human lives. Separations, loss, and grief seem to make up the greater part of life's emotional intensity.

Yet, something important happens in these moments of separation whether or not we plan them. We may always somehow benefit from the leave-takings, from the discontinuities and unravelings, especially if we see them as manifestations of the wisdom of psyche. From that perspective, they are natural and intentional; they fill our lives with adventure, surprise, discovery, even sorrow, and define for us what it means to be *us*. Leaving the safety and comfort of the womb is the first event of life. Birth is merely the first of a lifetime of leavings.

"What I think is that a good life is one hero journey after another. Over and over again, you are called to the realm of adventure, you are called to new horizons. Each time, there is the same problem: do I dare? And then if you do dare, the dangers are there, and help also, and the fulfillment or the fiasco. There's always the possibility of a fiasco. But there's also the possibility of bliss."

—PATHWAYS TO BLISS, *page 133*

One may refuse the call out of fear, or the departure might be interrupted for some reason, and the results are then radically different from those of the following the call."[4] The call comes from the unconscious, so refusing the call puts you in yet another unconscious situation that might be more difficult than the original conditions that summoned the call. Another call may be issued, and the adventure it portends may be that much more challenging, or, if the call is refused again, it may result in a deadening of life, an impoverishment of feeling, and a pervasive, enduring sense of missed opportunities.

In answering the call, one may encounter the shadow with its frightening aspects or disturbing obstacles. Additionally, one may even experience a kind of psychological dismemberment and then, Campbell says rather nonchalantly, "you enter the realm of adventure dead."[5] But if you have answered the call and crossed the threshold, as Campbell puts it, if it really is your adventure and appropriate to a deep psychic need, one that life has up to now been drawing you toward, "helpers will come along the way and provide magical aid."[6] Often, after receiving the magical aid, the sense of danger intensifies and one finds oneself in the Initiation phase of the journey, where one faces increasingly difficult trials. One is now moving into the deep unconscious, encountering its repressed, primitive content.

There are four types of initiatory trials in the initiatory stage of journey that, if handled successfully, result in a greater sense of wholeness, a greater sense of reconciliation to the conditions of life. The first, Campbell calls meeting the goddess.

Human beings can't receive the full truth of the goddess all at once, so the goddess meets us where we are. If we're not

Chapter VI: The Self as Hero

prepared, Campbell says, the encounter may seem harsh, but this meeting opens the door to the sacred marriage that serves as a metaphor for the union of opposites within. Jung believed the *hieros gamos*, the sacred marriage, was connected with the mythology of rebirth; it is a renewal of life and a conquering of death. "To put it in modern psychological language, this projection of the *hieros gamos* signifies the conjunction of conscious and unconscious, the transcendent function characteristic of the individuation process. Integration of the unconscious invariably has a healing effect."[7]

The second stage encountered on the road of trials is reconciliation—or, as Campbell puts it, atonement—with the father. Campbell explicitly states that "this trial is definitely a male rite of passage," which suggests to me that he is aware of the masculine bias in some aspects of the hero's journey paradigm, an issue that will be addressed in the following chapter.[8] The challenge of this trial is to bring the life one is living into accord with who one really is, to be open to the call of the passions, to live one's life with intention.

The third stage on the road of trials is that of "apotheosis," in which you realize that "you are what you are seeking."[9] One has, at this point, become transparent to the transcendent, a transparent Emersonian eyeball through which the ego vanishes. One realizes that one is part and parcel of the divine. There is a hint of this idea in the gospels, when Jesus remarks, "Is it not written in your law, 'I said, you are gods'?"[10]

One must remain patient while travelling this road of trials, because there will be times when one is tempted to push through all the obstacles without preparation or engagement, and simply seize the boon. Once this aggressive theft has occurred, there is no way to live harmoniously with the energies of life because you've wrenched something out of your deepest self that needed to be approached with wisdom and care and compassion in order to be given as a gift in at-one-ment, a sacred marriage of the deep self and consciousness, a fitting culmination to the effort spent in following one's bliss. But instead of bliss, this impulsive, aggressive trespass forces one to live with the regret of losing the Grail, one might say; of having forfeited one's bliss in exchange for violating the natural order of things and refusing to respect the conditions of life.

As mentioned before, the third and final stage of the hero's journey is the Return, and the Return is rather like a mirror image of the departure in that the hero returns by the same means by which he departed. If, for example, your departure was a night sea voyage, that is how you will return. The return symbolizes the successful achievement of your own potential. The challenges one previously faced along the road of trials are metaphors for what Campbell describes in *The Hero with a Thousand Faces* as "the agony of breaking through personal limitations [which] is the agony of spiritual growth."[11]

Furthermore, returning with the boon may be even more difficult than discovering it. Campbell offers his own story as an example to illustrate how one might be able to find a small niche in which to live out one's passion until more and more of the world discovers that one has something to offer, something the world didn't even know it needed.

Campbell ends this chapter beautifully with a reference to T.S. Eliot's poem, "The Love Song of J. Alfred Prufrock," in which

the angst-ridden Prufrock repeatedly asks the question, "Do I dare?" in various situations such as descending the stairs, eating a peach, and most poignantly, "Do I dare / Disturb the universe?" What we mostly fail to understand is that the universe wants to be disturbed, and it wants to be disturbed by us! The heroic journey is not about personalized success nor is it entirely about the fulfilment of ourselves as individuals; the hero's journey also places each of us in the role of an agent working toward the fulfilment of the universe itself.

Of course, "there's always the possibility of a fiasco. But there's also the possibility of bliss."[12]

Points of Interest

MORE ON SCHOPENHAUER

Since he read Schopenhauer in German, Campbell gives a literal translation of Schopenhauer's essay titled "On an Apparent Intention in the Fate of the Individual."[13] In other translations, the title is commonly rendered as "Transcendent Speculation on the Apparent Deliberateness in the Fate of the Individual," and may be found in a book of Schopenhauer's writing called *Parerga and Paralipomena: A Collection of Philosophical Essays*. Here is the Schopenhauer excerpt that Campbell refers to in Chapter VI:

> Consequently, all the events in a man's life are connected in two fundamentally different ways; first in the objective causal connection of the course of nature, secondly in a subjective connection that exists only in reference to

the individual who experiences them. It is as subjective as his own dreams, yet in him their succession and content are likewise necessarily determined, but in the manner in which the succession of the scenes of a drama is determined by the plan of the poet.[14]

In the same essay, Schopenhauer notes how often, when we've carefully mapped out a plan for our lives and set out to pursue it, we are forced to watch the machinery of fate crush it. He writes that we often discover in retrospect that our plan wasn't suited to our true welfare, and that by overturning it, fate places us on our rightful path. And if we persist in doggedly pursuing our plan just the same, fate is likely to rain down even heavier blows upon us because if we succeed in forcing the issue, it would "tend merely to our harm and undoing." Schopenhauer quotes a Latin axiom, "*ducunt volentem fata, nolentem trahunt*": Fate leads the willing, but drags along the unwilling. From Schopenhauer's perspective, fate isn't simply random chance; it is a manifestation of Will.[15] The Will that maintains the phenomenon of the universe is the same Will that lives in and operates on each of us. Schopenhauer is an early adopter of determinism, believing that humans are incapable of free will. He feels we need to believe we possess free will in order to maintain concepts such as moral responsibility.

THE BOON

The word *boon* comes from the old Norse *bon*, which meant a prayer, and the Proto-Germanic *boniz*, which denoted a prayer or petition, as well as *bannan*, which meant to summon. Gradually *boon* evolved to mean a favor or something asked for,

"Well, there are monsters round about, and the mother tells them, 'Don't go far from the house. You may go eastward, southward, and westward, but don't go north.' Of course, they go north. How are you going to change the situation unless you break the rules? Her proscription is the call to adventure."

—PATHWAYS TO BLISS, *page 127*

and eventually to mean a good thing received, a benefit enjoyed. A boon, then, is something given that the world desperately needs, that humankind cries out for and prays to receive. The trouble is that the world and those in it often don't know they need the hero's boon. In the face of such apathy the hero may be tempted to abandon the whole project.

THE PSYCHOLOGICAL IMPACT OF MYTH

Ancient myths can help us understand contemporary psychology. The myths depict important aspects of our experience. For example, being turned to ashes and then reborn is a metaphor for psychological discovery and recovery. That particular hero's journey is an image of diving deep within oneself to discover the hidden treasures of wholeness and a unified self, then returning to society and culture with the creative energy of renewal and rebirth. And even though our lives may be turned to ashes, those ashes "become diffused through time and space ... forming at last a part of every shore the world over."[16]

Complementary Reading from Campbell's Work

Campbell, Joseph. *The Hero with a Thousand Faces*. New World Library, 2008.

Campbell, Joseph, and Henry Morton Robinson. *A Skeleton Key to Finnegans Wake: Unlocking James Joyce's Masterwork*. New World Library, 2005.

Further Reading

Cousineau, Phil (editor). *The Hero's Journey: Joseph Campbell on His Life and Work.* New World Library, 2003.

Flaubert, Gustav. *A Sentimental Education: The Story of a Young Man.* Oxford World's Classics, 2000.

Jung, C.G. *The Undiscovered Self: The Dilemma of the Individual in Modern Society.* Berkley, 2006.

Towles, Amor. *A Gentleman in Moscow.* Viking, 2016.

Discussion Questions

- What did James Joyce, and by extension Joseph Campbell, mean by the term *monomyth*? What do you see as the strengths and limitations of that term?

- What are the three main stages of the hero's adventure? What aspects of your life can you apply them to?

- Can one decide not to have a hero's adventure? And if so, why might somebody make that choice? What might be the results of that choice?

Essay Topics

- Research and analyze how a heroine's journey might be similar to or different from a hero's journey as Campbell describes it. How might we degender the adventure?

"This is what Joyce called the monomyth: an archetypal story that springs from the collective unconscious. Its motifs can appear not only in myth and literature, but, if you are sensitive to it, in the working out of the plot of your own life."

—PATHWAYS TO BLISS, *page 112-113*

- Why might a hero who has successfully "completed" the adventure refuse to return? Explore the benefits and drawbacks of choosing to return—or not.

- Campbell says that his idea of a good life is one hero's adventure after another. Research what two other philosophers, psychologists, or novelists consider to be a good life, and compare their views with Campbell's. Which do you find most compelling, and why?

Creative Prompts

- Think of an experience you have had that has the three stages Separation, Initiation, and Return. Now tell the story of that experience using characters from "The Frog Prince" instead of from your actual life.

- Now write the same story using any characters you like, except put it into a series of three limericks, one each for the Separation, Initiation, and Return.

- Design, prepare, and share a meal that tells this same story.

NOTES

1 I believe there is no question but that the hero's journey has a decidedly masculine perspective, but it should not be taken to mean that women cannot have a heroic journey. As we will see, Joseph Campbell, with the aid of his audience, addresses this issue in Chapter VII of *Pathways to Bliss*. One may also read Maureen Murdock's *The Heroine's Journey* (Shambhala,

2020) and Valerie Estelle Frankle's *From Girl to Goddess: The Heroine's Journey Through Myth and Legend* (McFarland, 2014) for conceptualizations of the hero's journey from a feminine perspective.

2 Joseph Campbell, *Pathways to Bliss*, 113.

3 Ibid, 113.

4 Ibid, 113.

5 Ibid, 115.

6 Ibid, 116.

7 C.G. Jung, *Symbols of Transformation*, trans. R.F.C. Hull (Routledge, 2014), §672.

8 Joseph Campbell, *Pathways to Bliss*, 117.

9 Ibid, 118.

10 John 10: 34–36.

11 Joseph Campbell, *The Hero with a Thousand Faces* (New World Library, 2008), 164.

12 Joseph Campbell, *Pathways to Bliss*, 133.

13 Ibid, 112.

14 Arthur Schopenhauer, "Transcendent Speculation on the Apparent Deliberateness in the Fate of the Individual," *Parerga and Paralipomena* (Cambridge University Press, 2016), 220.

15 Schopenhauer discusses this in his book, *Will in Die Welt als Wille und Vorstellung*, or in English, *The World as Will and Representation* (Dover, 1966).

16 I've borrowed this exquisitely beautiful line from Herman Melville's *Moby Dick* (Norton, 2002), 136.

Chapter VII
Dialogues

Chapter Summary

This chapter contains a selection of questions and answers from some of the lectures from which this volume was created. These questions and Campbell's responses shine more light on some of the ideas previously mentioned in the book such as the functions of rites and ritual, and particularly the question of how women experience the hero's journey.

First, let's look at ritual. When you participate in a ritual, Campbell notes that:

> You are acting not in terms of your individual, personal life but with the sense of yourself as the priest, so to say, of a cosmic power which is operating through you, which we all are in circumstances, and the problem is to balance yourself against that and have a personality at the same time.[1]

Becoming aware of the cosmic power operating through oneself while simultaneously being aware of oneself as a personality is a very difficult balancing act. We tend to be aware of one role or situation at a time but, as Campbell discussed in Chapter IV, the risk of creating an imbalanced, over-identified psyche can invite a troubling enantiodromia. Participating in ritual can be a helpful way to maintain psychic balance. In a ritual one acts as if one is a god, an animal, or an energetic force, while at the same time the ritual performer knows they are not actually what they are pretending to be.

In a lecture on the function of ritual,[2] Campbell remarks on our tendency to find ourselves by imitating others. Children imitate parents, hunting cultures wear animal masks and skins imitating the sacred animal, planting cultures bury their dead in the ground as if expecting a new life to sprout. Campbell adds, "At some point you have to wonder, to what degree is this a game?" This suggests that life is playful, a game, perhaps that life is *a* play, and we are merely actors who have forgotten we're playing roles. The metaphor of play or performance leads to the impression that there is much more to life than what we experience on a material plane. If there could be life of some kind outside the game, outside the theaters in which we perform, well, that must be the real life that we imitate.

This real life and one's true nature are sometimes revealed in a transcendent moment—an iridescent, ephemeral, transparent experience in which some deep truth dispels existential dread, and we understand that there is more to life than the facts determined by biology and our limited cognitive faculty. For example, we know many forms of energy that are invisible to us can be perceived by other animals. Some hear sounds and see light well outside the range of human perception. Some animals have built-in compasses that align their bodies with the north-south axis of the earth's magnetic field.

In my opinion, the most interesting question of this chapter is: "Can you talk about the woman's hero journey? Is it the same as for a man?"[3] Campbell's answer to the question shows that he has given some thought to this issue, although from our perspective today his views and his language sound a bit dated, as they are:

"But the simple tasks of our life, when you're doing them because they're a function or factor in the life that you love and have chosen and have given yourself, then they don't weigh you down."

—PATHWAYS TO BLISS, *page 158*

> All of the great mythologies and much of the mythic storytelling of the world are from the male point of view. When I was writing *The Hero with a Thousand Faces* and wanted to bring female heroes in, I had to go to the fairy tales. These were told by women to children, you know, and you get a different perspective. It was men who got involved in spinning most of the great myths. The women were too busy; they had too damn much to do to sit around thinking about stories.[4]

It's important to note that this statement is a broad generalization that does not always hold up. For example, the ancient Sumerian priestess and princess Enheduanna wrote truly great myths in the form of poetry about the goddess Inanna. And although I don't believe Campbell intended it, his statement does sound dismissive of women's experience, comparing "great myths" to seemingly lesser fairy tales for children. Today we know that value judgments like these limit more than amplify our understanding.

Campbell goes on to speculate that, for women, the masculine represents "the agent of the feminine power directed toward a certain specific kind of functioning." Males, however, lack "that recall to nature, to the female nature that there is automatically in the female body."[5] Later, he remarks that a certain kind of Janist yoga was not recommended for women because it was a yoga intended to "cancel nature altogether" so that one may die without any attachment whatsoever to life. The reason that this yoga is not to be engaged by women, Campbell explains, is that "there is too much life in [women's] bodies."[6]

A woman[7] in the audience holds Campbell's feet to the fire, saying:

> Woman: I do have a little bit of a bone to pick with you, because I do feel that there is a traditional part of you, part of you personally, that does see the female as different from the male, and I'm not sure that I agree.
>
> Campbell: Well, these are two ways of experiencing, I would say, that's all. I would like for about ten minutes actually to be a female, just to know what the difference is.[8]

And yet, later in the exchange Campbell insists that women don't have to be tied to their biology, that they have the same vocational freedom as men do.

The lectures comprising *Pathways to Bliss* were given between 1962 and 1983. Campbell first published *Hero* in 1949. Betty Freidan's *The Feminine Mystique* wasn't published until 1963. Second-wave feminism and the discussion of the role of women, gender norms, and cultural inequalities didn't emerge in America until the 1960s. It is fascinating to see how Campbell is willing to roll with and incorporate these ideas rather than take refuge in traditional gender norms and classically Jungian conceptions of the anima/animus archetype that today, frankly, seem reductively gendered and anachronistic.

Take, for instance, the idea that consciousness is associated with the masculine and the unconscious with the feminine. There is a tendency to think that consciousness, which was traditionally considered masculine, is good and stable, while the unconscious, traditionally associated with the feminine, implies problematic unpredictability. I find it much more useful to talk about specific attributes of consciousness rather than to identify it with gendered labels. Additionally, masculinity and

Chapter VII: Dialogues

femininity are obviously not the only two options for gender expression. Finally, in Campbell's exchanges with his audience, we see that focusing too much on masculinity and femininity tends to unnecessarily complicate the issue and diminishes our ability to understand and reflect upon the realities of living, reacting, thinking, and behaving as human beings, rather than as women and men. The deeper, more problematic aspects of all our relationships are obscured by focusing too intently on psychological issues from a rigidly gendered perspective.

Campbell emphasizes that "The important thing, however, is not for the masculine to be the dominant or the feminine to be dominant; what is to be dominant is the *coniunctio oppositorum*, the conjunction of the two."[9] He ultimately drives home the point that, regardless of gender, the hero's journey consists of a psychological move into one's own depths with the goal to revitalize deadened feeling; integrate scattered, compartmentalized self-knowledge; and to emerge more whole, more self-directed, more generously disposed to the conditions of living and to life itself, even in its threatening aspects and drudgery.

Campbell points out that "the adventure is always reckless ... And that goes even for the simple things I do ..."[10] The drudgery of housework, or rewriting a book, or riding a subway home after an exhausting day's work can become heroic acts. "... This is when you bring that factor of love in," Campbell says. As long as doing the dishes is not regarded as an act of love, or a physical manifestation of loving the life you have, doing the dishes feels oppressive. But, "When you love the dishes and you think about what they mean in your life ... your family's sustenance ... then it's all transformed into metaphor and you're free."[11] And that freedom, after all, is the entire *raison d'etre* for the heroic journey in the first place.

143

"When Saint Paul says, 'I live now; not I, but Christ liveth in me,' that's one thing. It's another thing to put the Christ up on a mountain. This is a big problem in life: what do you do with your Christ when he comes along? Do you take that image ... and let it become the motivating force for your life, or do you put it up there and make a war cry out of it?"

—PATHWAYS TO BLISS, *pages 137-138*

Chapter VII: Dialogues

Points of Interest

LIFE AS A GAME

Understanding life as a game is, I think, one of the important keys to understanding Joseph Campbell's work and his life. It's how he was able to "participate joyfully in the sorrows of the world." Choosing to live in joy and see life as a game exemplifies what Campbell calls the "aristocratic spirit," which engages life nobly, honestly, and courageously, even while knowing that our experience of life is not the ultimate experience, but rather is a metaphor, a play. The things that are sorrowful, horrifying, and even joyful are merely passing forms, and as such, all part of the cosmic game of hide and seek. "We cannot cure the world of sorrows," Campbell says, "but we can choose to live in joy."[12]

GENDER, NATURE, AND CULTURE

Tying women to their biological experiences is problematic, to say the least. In her brilliant, and now classic, 1974 essay "Is Female to Male as Nature is to Culture?"[13] Sherry B. Ortner argues that women have been seen as the symbol of something every culture demeans and determines to be of less value than the culture itself:

> Every culture, or, generically, "culture," is engaged in the process of generating and sustaining systems of meaningful forms (symbols, artifacts, etc.) by means of which humanity transcends the givens of natural existence, bends them to its purposes, controls them in its interest. We may thus broadly equate culture with the notion of human consciousness, or with the products of human consciousness (i.e., systems

of thought and technology), by means of which humanity attempts to assert control over nature.[14]

Women, Ortner argues, come to symbolize nature because bodily functions like childbirth and menstruation seem to suggest a closer relationship to the rhythms of nature than does a man's biology, which in fact seems to free him from it so that he may engage in the enterprise of building culture. Also, childbearing often leads to social roles that are domestically oriented, roles that are deemed to be of a lower order, and as a result women are often granted a lower order of cultural esteem.

In other words, woman's body seems to doom her to mere reproduction of life; the male, in contrast, lacking natural creative functions, must (or has the opportunity to) assert his creativity externally, "artificially," through the medium of technology and symbols. In so doing, he creates relatively lasting, eternal, transcendent objects, while the woman creates only perishables—human beings.[15]

Perhaps most salient for this discussion is the belief that culture must subdue and dominate nature, which, if women are identified with nature, leads to the false conclusion that men must similarly dominate women.

Complementary Reading from Campbell's Works

Campbell, Joseph, and Safron Rossi (editor). *Goddesses: Mysteries of the Feminine Divine*. New World Library, 2013.

Campbell, Joseph. *Masks of God, Vol. 3: Occidental Mythology.* New World Library, 2022.

Further Reading

Murdock, Maureen. *The Heroine's Journey.* Shambhala, 1990.

Rosaldo, M.Z., and L. Lamphere (editors). *Women, Culture, and Society.* Stanford University Press, 1974.

Adichie, Chimamanda Ngozi. *We Should All Be Feminists.* Anchor Books, 2015.

Jung, C.G. *Psychological Types.* Routledge, 2016.

Discussion Questions

- What does Joseph Campbell mean by "killing the dragon?" Give a few examples of this from your own life.

- On page 139 of *Pathways to Bliss*, Campbell discusses transcending dualism. What do you think that means, and how might one accomplish that?

- Describe how you think the heroine's journey might differ from the hero's journey.

"Sometimes the drudgery itself can become part of the hero deed. The point is not to get stuck in the drudgery but to use it to free you."

—PATHWAYS TO BLISS, *page 165*

Essay Topics

- Choose one of your favorite games: a computer game, board game, or sport. Write about how this game works well as a metaphor for life, and about where the metaphor breaks down.

- Compare and contrast the hero's journey with the heroine's journey.

- In Greek mythology, the prophet Tiresias was transformed into a woman for seven years. Research this myth, and write an essay about what you think he might have learned.

Creative Prompts

If you could ask Joseph Campbell a question, what would it be? Write the dialogue for a scene where you ask the question, he answers, and you have a conversation about it.

NOTES

1 Joseph Campbell, *Pathways to Bliss*, 139.
2 You can find this lecture as Episode 3 on the Joseph Campbell Foundation's flagship podcast, *Pathways with Joseph Campbell*, which I am honored and delighted to host. Find it at jcf.org or your favorite podcast hosting site.
3 Joseph Campbell, *Pathways to Bliss*, 145.
4 Ibid, 145.
5 Ibid, 147.

6 Ibid, 148.
7 In this chapter, the people asking questions of Campbell are not identified and remain anonymous in the text.
8 Joseph Campbell, *Pathways to Bliss*, 148.
9 Ibid, 142.
10 Ibid, 156.
11 Ibid, 158.
12 Joseph Campbell, *A Joseph Campbell Companion: Reflections on the Art of Living* (Joseph Campbell Foundation, 2011), 17.
13 This paper really is a must-read. Even though as of this writing it is 47 years old, it still has value to a contemporary reader, and a great deal to offer a reader of Campbell's works, as it is of a similar vintage even though the authors are not.
14 Sherry B. Ortner, "Is Female to Male as Nature is to Culture?," in *Woman, Culture, and Society*, ed. Michelle Zimbalist Rosaldo (Stanford University Press, 1974), 72.
15 Ibid, 75.

Final Thoughts from Bradley Olson, PhD

Reflecting on the completion of this study guide, I feel privileged and honored to have been able to comment upon the work of Joseph Campbell. I am forever indebted to Robert Walter, a founder, and for more than three decades the president, of the Joseph Campbell Foundation, for his encouragement and support in the creative endeavors with which I've been involved at JCF, but most importantly for his friendship. I'm also grateful to Joanna Gardner for the remarkable editing talents she has brought to bear on not only this book, but the entire Skeleton Key Study Guide series. And to my dear Roxanne, who has been the bliss I've followed for nearly thirty-four years.

I'm also grateful for the central, enriching role that myth has played in my life with its power to delight, educate, console, inspire, and illuminate, while touching, as Campbell has said, the deepest centers of human motivation. Myth helps me to recognize and understand the continually unfolding archetypal energies and forms and their impact on the lives of modern individuals, and perhaps more importantly, on my own life. But I also recognize that while those "deep centers of motivation" can employ myth in ways that are life enhancing, the power of myth may be just as easily employed to disenfranchise and dehumanize others. Myth is a world-building tool, and we can't afford to lose touch with its ironic and metaphorical nature, for when myth is literalized, the worlds we create seem always to careen toward the dystopian.

I believe that psychology, art, literature, and culture studies lend understanding and relevance to myth, just as myth lends understanding and relevance to psychology, art, literature, and culture studies. This essential reciprocity moves one's understanding toward a deep relationship with beauty, with the fascinating mystery of existence, with dignity and creativity—in short, with life itself.

Finally, but certainly not exhaustively, I believe that the study of myth is not a coherent subject and is open to many interpretations and approaches, some of them confusing and perhaps even contradictory. But myth is, for me, more a mode of thinking or imagining rather than merely a collection of old stories, ancient wisdom, sacred rituals, or a particular body of knowledge. Myth extends itself into practically every domain of life and influences nearly every human thought and endeavor. If myths are, as Campbell once suggested, public dreams, then the study of myth is the royal road that leads to the understanding of the human heart.

About Joseph Campbell

Joseph Campbell was an American author and teacher best known for his work in the field of comparative mythology. He was born in New York City in 1904, and from early childhood he became interested in mythology. He loved to read books about Indigenous American cultures, and frequently visited the American Museum of Natural History in New York, where he was fascinated by the museum's collection of totem poles. Campbell was educated at Columbia University, where he specialized in medieval literature, and, after earning a master's degree, continued his studies at universities in Paris and Munich. While abroad he was influenced by the art of Pablo Picasso and Henri Matisse, the novels of James Joyce and Thomas Mann, and the psychological studies of Sigmund Freud and Carl Jung. These encounters led to Campbell's theory that all myths and epics are linked in the human psyche, and that they are cultural manifestations of the need to explain social, cosmological, and spiritual realities.

After a period in California, where he encountered John Steinbeck and the biologist Ed Ricketts, Campbell taught at the Canterbury School, and then, in 1934, joined the literature department at Sarah Lawrence College, a post he retained for many years. During the 1940s and '50s, he helped Swami Nikhilananda to translate the Upaniṣads and *The Gospel of Sri Ramakrishna*. He also edited works by the German scholar Heinrich Zimmer on Indian art, myths, and philosophy. In 1944, with Henry Morton Robinson, Campbell published *A Skeleton Key to Finnegans Wake*. His first original work, *The Hero with a Thousand Faces*, came out in 1949 and was immediately well received; in time, it became acclaimed as a classic. In this study of the "myth of the hero," Campbell asserted that there is a single pattern of heroic journey and that all cultures share this essential pattern in their various heroic myths. In his book he also outlined the basic conditions, stages, and results of the archetypal hero's journey.

Joseph Campbell died in 1987. In 1988, a series of television interviews with Bill Moyers, *The Power of Myth*, introduced Campbell's views to millions of people.

About the Author

Bradley Olson, PhD, a former police officer, is now a writer and depth psychologist in private practice in Flagstaff, Arizona. Dr. Olson serves as the publications director at the Joseph Campbell Foundation, where he also edits and contributes to the popular MythBlast series and hosts the Foundation's flagship podcast, *Pathways with Joseph Campbell.*

For more about Dr. Olson's MythBlasts, podcasts, and professional activities, visit jcf.org and bradleyolsonphd.com.

About the Joseph Campbell Foundation

The Joseph Campbell Foundation invites you to experience the power of myth. Building on the work of Joseph Campbell, we offer resources and community for those who hear the call to adventure.

For more information about Joseph Campbell and the Joseph Campbell Foundation, contact:

Joseph Campbell Foundation
www.jcf.org

www.ingramcontent.com/pod-product-compliance
Lightning Source LLC
Chambersburg PA
CBHW061808070526
44586CB00024B/2761